Aldo Giannini

EAT & LOVE TUSCANY

The TUSCAN COOKBOOK

ALDO GIANNINI

EAT & LOVE TUSCANY

The TUSCAN COOKBOOK

TABLE
OF CONTENTS

FOREWORD

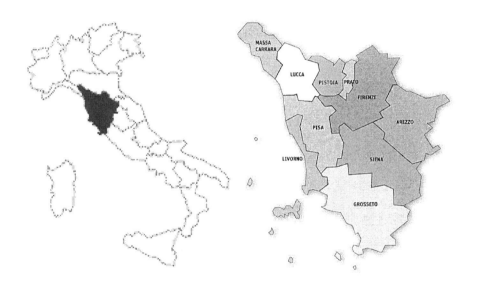

Tuscan cuisine is famous, appreciated all over the world.

It is rich in natural ingredients, genuine traditional products, simple and unique regional dishes, and excellent wine like the Chianti Classico or the Brunello of Montalcino.

Extra virgin olive oil of excellent quality is an important ingredient of almost every tuscan dish.

A typical Tuscan meal usually starts with an antipasto of cured meat (prosciutto, lard from "Colonnata" and different types of sausages), or crostini di fegato, thin slices of lightly toasted bread spread with a chicken liver pate, or fettunta, a grilled slice of bread with garlic, olive oil and salt. Tuscans are also fond of their soups like the ribollita or pappa al pomodoro.

Meals are usually served accompanied by bread. But, unlike the bread found in other parts of Italy, in the Tuscan region, the bread is usually made without adding salt.

This tradition dates back to the 16th century when Tuscany faced a salt shortage and a tax was put on salt, changing the way locals were making bread.

As every other Italian region, Tuscany has its own local or regional dishes like lampredotto sandwich, tagliatelle al tartufo, pappardelle alla lepre, bistecca alla fiorentina or cacciuco alla livornese, etc.

ANTIPASTI
(STARTERS)

CROSTINI
TOASTED BREAD SLICES
WITH TOPPINGS

Ingredients

bread slices
(pane toscano "per crostini")
8-12
topping

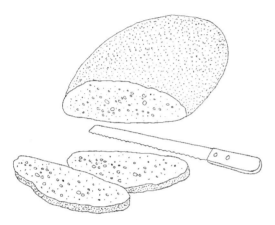

Preparation

Prepare the topping using the chosen ingredients. Spread the topping over the bread slices, already moderately toasted, but still warm.

Serve the seasoned bread slice or bake them breafly in a preheated oven.

BLACK CROSTINI
(CHICKEN LIVER CROSTINI)
Crostini neri toscani,
crostini toscani,
crostini ai fegatini di pollo

In a pan fry gently chopped onions. Then add the minced sage and the chicken livers. Cook over moderate heat. Every now and then pour in some dry white wine or, even better, the vinsanto or marsala wine.

When the chicken livers are done or almost done, take them out and chop them coarsly, adding the desolted anchovy fillets and capers, in moderate quantities, mincing and mixing the ingredients.

Put the mixture back on the stove and continue cooking for another 1-2 minutes, over very moderate heat. From time to time pour in some meat soup or water.

This step is not necessary, meaning that you can consider the patè done without further cooking.

Season the chicken liver patè with salt and pepper.

Optional ingredients: spleen, rabbit liver, parsley, celery, lard (lardo di Colonnata), butter, flour, garlic, bread crumbs, rosemary, ground meat, tomato paste, red wine, lemon juice or peel, bay leaves, sausage meat, onions, nutmeg, pimento (pementa, pepe garofanato), carrot, smoked ham, thyme, aceto balsamico, cream, peperoncino.

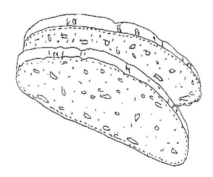

Optional proceeding: In the end, immersion blender may be used to prepare a cream or pasta consistency of the topping mixture.

Possible omissions: sage, onions.

Note: Typical topping used for the crostinis across the region.

Optional proceeding: The toasted bread slices may be sligtly dipped into a meat or vegetable soup, before spreading the topping.

WHITE CROSTINI
Crostini bianchi

The topping for the white crostini is prepared by mixing the butter and cheese (provolone, mozzarella, brie, pecorino, grana padano or other) and, if possible, some white truffles.

MUSHROOM CROSTINI
Crostini ai funghi

Slice the mushrooms (porcini or others). Fry them gently in a pan, with olive oil and other ingredients, such as garlic, nepittela (an italian herb, calamint), tomatoes or tomato paste, sausages, and salt and pepper. Cook over moderate heat for 10-15 minutes. At the end add some minced capers and chopped parsley.

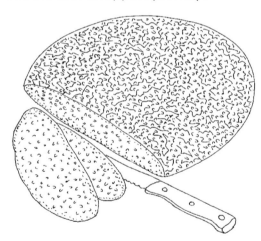

SHRIMP AND MUSSEL CROSTINI
Crostini ai gamberi e cozze

Boil the shrimp and mussel meat.

In a bowl mix the boiled shrimp and mussel meat, crushed garlic, minced parsley, bread crumbs, olive oil, salt and pepper, maybe even chopped peperoncino.

TUSCAN CALE AND LARD CROSTINI
Crostini
con cavolo nero e lardo

Boil the leaves of the Tuscan cale. Drain the well cooked cale leaves and mince them. Add some olive oil, salt and pepper. Spread the topping mix over the crostini surface and lay over the topping a thin slice of the lard or pancetta.

LEEK AND GORGONZOLA CROSTINI
Crostini ai porri e gorgonzola

Clean and then chop the leeks. In a pan fry them gently with olive oil. Add some chopped peperoncino (or paprica powder) and season with salt. Pour in dry white wine and let it almost evaporate.

Dispose bread slices in a baking pan. On each slice spread the prepared topping and lay also slices of gorgonzola cheese.

Preheat the oven to 180°. Put the pan into the preheated oven and bake until the cheese melts.

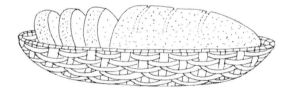

LARDO DI COLONNATA CROSTINI
Crostini al lardo di Colonnata

In bowl mix the finely chopped lard, crushed garlic, white vinegar, rosemary, salt and pepper. Spread the topping over the toasted bread slices.

Different method: Spread over the toasted bread slices some olive oil and crushed garlic. Lay over each seasoned slice a few slices of lard.

COD FISH CROSTINI
Crostini di baccalà mantecato

Soak the dried cod fish in water for 3-4 days, changing the water daily. Then cook the cod fish in fresh water.

Clean the cooked fish, removing the skin and the bones) and cut the meat into pieces. Then beat the fish meat until it becomes a pulp. Add the minced parsley and garlic. After that, drizzle and stir in the oil. Season with salt and (freshly ground) pepper.

Spread the prepared topping over the toasted bread slices.

Optional herbs and spices: milk, cinnamon, green olives.

RED CROSTINI
Crostini rossi

In a small bowl soak the inner part of of 200 g of a bread loaf, best of the whole wheat bread, for 10-15 minutes, in vinegar. After that, squeeze the bread.

In another, larger bowl mix well the chopped tomatoes (2-3), 1 tbsp of capers, chopped parsley, crushed garlic, 3-4 tbsp of olive oil, salt and pepper. Thyme or basil leaves may be added.

Spread the prepared topping over the toasted bread slices.

CHEESE AND SAUSAGE CROSTINI
Crostini stracchino e salsiccia

In a bowl mix 200 g of stracchino cheese and the chopped peeled sausages. Then spread the prepared topping over the toasted bread slices.

Note: Stracchino, also known as crescenza is a type of Italian cow's milk cheese. It is eaten very young, has a very soft, creamy texture and a mild and delicate flavour.

Optional ingredients: The stracchino cheese may be supstituted with mozzarella or other type of soft cheese.

Optional herbs and spices: sage, rosemary, paprica.

CROSTINI WITH THE GARFAGNANA RED SAUCE
Crostini alla salsa rossa della Garfagnana

In a bowl mix the crumbled bay leaves (4-7), crushed garlic cloves (1-2), capers (7-15), minced salted enchovy fillets (5-15), or salted enchovy paste, some lemon juice, concentrated tomato paste (200-300 g), or tomato passata, olive oil 5-8 tbsp, salt.

Vinegar or aceto balsamico, or peperoncino or pepper may be added.

Spread the prepared topping over the toasted bread slices.

CROSTINI, CROSTONI, PANE BRUSCATO AND BRUSCHETTE (the difference)

Basically it is the same thing - a slice of bread, toasted and seasoned with a topping, or seasoned first and then baked briefly.

TUSCAN BREAD
PANE TOSCANO
PANE SCIAPO, PANE SCIOCCO

What makes the Tuscan bread so particular is the absence of salt. This tradition dates back to the 16th century when Tuscany faced a salt shortage and a tax was put on salt, which made the salt also too expensive to use for making bread.

It is also a fact that the Tuscan type of bread, the unsalted bread, provides an ideal compensation for the robust and savory flavors of Tuscan food: salamis such as finocchiona, cheese like the sheep cheese from Pienza, crostini, bruschette, lampredotto and the perfect link with soups like ribollita or pappa al pomodoro.

PANIGACCI

Panigaccio is a type of thin, round, flat bread, made without yeast, prepared simply, with flour, water and salt and traditionally cooked in hot dishes, called testi.

Serve the panigacci hot with prosciutto, salami and cheese, even with basil pesto.

There is even a festival dedicated to the dish which takes place in Podenzana and is called the Sagra del Panigaccio.

COVACCINO

Covaccino is a thin bread type, made with yeast, baked in a wood oven, seasoned with oil and salt, sometimes even rosemary, and eaten alone or with cured meat and cheese, often in sandwiches.

CIABATTA

Ciabatta is a flattened type of bread, couple of centimetres high, shaped as a slipper, hence the name.

SCHIACCIATA

Schiacciata is a flat type of bread, only a centimetre or two high, similar to focaccia. In some parts of Tuscany it is called ciaccino.

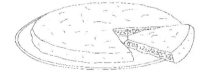

This type of flatbread is either baked crunchy or soft with fillings. Stuffing may include fresh or cured meats, greaves, cheese or vegetables.

eat and love Tuscany

FOCACCIA

Focaccia is similar to schiacciata. The dough is often seasoned with rosemary.

In the focaccia dough the sage can substitute the rosemary.

FETTUNTA

Ingredients

toasted bread slices 8-12
olio d'oliva 3-4 cucchiai
aglio 2-3 spicchi
sale, pepe

Preparation

Rub each toasted bread slice with crushed garlic. Spread also some olive oil. Season with salt and pepper.

PECORINO ALL'ETRUSCA

Ingredients

sheep cheese
(pecorino etrusco,
pecorino di Pienza
or other)
250 g
pine nuts 10-20 g
olive oil 4-5 tbsp
aceto balsamico
honey 1 tbsp
salt

Preparation

In a bowl mix well the aceto balsamico, honey, minced pine nuts, olive oil and salt.

Season the pecorino slices with the prepared sauce.

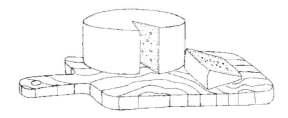

Optional ingredients: cooked prosciutto ham.

COCCOLI

Ingredients

flour 500 g
brewer's yeast 40-50 g
olive oil, butter or lard
3-5 tbsp
water, skimmed milk
or vegetable soup
400-500 ml
frying oil
salet

Preparation

Dissolve the yeast in the chosen liquid and then pour it in the center of the flour. Add the fat, salt and the remaining liquid, kneading the dough.

Cover the dough with a cloth and let it rest for a couple of hours.

After that, divide the dough into smaller parts and form balls or small cylinders.

Fry the coccoli in abundant hot oil.

Note: Tuscans love to eat the savory fritters called coccoli, accompanied by cured ham cut into very thin slices and cheese (stracchino or al.), or cheese only.

CIAFFAGNONI
CRESPELLE DI MANCIANO

CIAFFAGNONI are pancakes prepared with flour, eggs, water and salt, very thin, seasoned with Tuscan pecorino cheese.

This is a specialty of Manciano.

PANCROCINO

Cut 2.5-3 cm thick slices of bread from the centre of a loaf. Put them on a grill.

Turning the bread slices in different directions several times gives them the criss-cross pattern on both sides. This pattern gave them their name.

Toast the bread slices until they are crisp on the outside but still soft in the middle.

While the bread is on the grill, put 4-5 tbsp of oil in a blender together with a couple of tomatoes, 2-3 onions, some parsley, 1-2 garlic cloves and salt and pepper. Blend until the ingredients turn into a paste.

Separately slice the 2-3 tomatoes and a couple of onions.

Rub each of the toasted bread slices with crushed garlic and season with olive oil. Then spread over the toasted bread slices the prepared topping. After that put on the tomato slices and then the onion slices.

This is a specialty of the Tuscan Maremma region.

eat and love Tuscany

SOUP

RIBOLLITA

Ingredients

bread 4-8 slices
tuscan kale (cavolo nero), broccoli,
leaf cabbage, couliflower
300-400 g
tomatoes 100-250 g
beans 200-250 g
olive oil 4-5 tbsp
garlic 1-2 cloves
salt, pepper
carrots 1-2
onions 1-2
celery 1-2
parsley

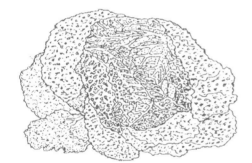

Preparation

Boil the soaked beans. With the kale, tomatoes and herbs, prepare a soup. Pass a third of the vegetables, extracted from the soup, through a vegetable mill, and also pass two thirds of the boiled beans.

Put the vegetable purée back in the pot with the soup, pour the cream of the beans and the remaining whole beans. Stir and cook for another 4-5 minutes.

Pour a ladle of vegetable soup into each bowl of terracota, arrange the slices of bread and cover them with the vegetables. Sprinkle with oil and pepper. Serve immediately.

Optional ingredients: broccoli, peas, bay leaves, basil, sage, potatoes, leeks, chard, thyme, rosemary.

Optional proceeding: Toast the slices of bread. You can rub them with garlic.

Different method: Place the slices of bread in an oven dish. Pour over the soup and the boiled beans. Cover with onion cut into thin slices and sprinkle with oil. Bake for 5-6 minutes. Remove the ribollita from the oven and let it rest for 5-10 minutes.

Notes: Traditionally, to prepare this dish (whose name means "boiled again"), typical of the Tuscan cuisine, advanced cooked vegetables were used.

PAPPA AL POMODORO

Ingredients

vegetable soup 1 litre
tomatoes 700-800 g
bread 300-400 g
olive oil 4-5 tbsp
garlic 2-3 cloves
onion 1 small
salt, pepper

Preparation

Peel the tomatoes and cut them into

small pieces. Peel the garlic and onion and mince them finely. Cut the bread into cubes.

In a pot, over low heat, brown the onion in the oil and then add the garlic. Put in the tomatoes and cook for 20 minutes over medium heat.

Then add salt and pepper and the bread. Sprinkle with the boiling soup. Continue cooking for another 20-25 minutes over low heat. At the end of cooking, crush everything. Season with salt and pepper. Remove the "pappa" from the heat, let it rest for 10-15 minutes and then serve it, warm or cold.

Optional ingredients: sugar, carrots, celery, leeks.

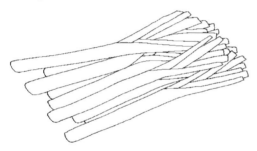

Optional ingredients at the end: olive oil, pepper, basil, rosemary.

Optional proceeding: Toast the slices of bread (chopped). You can rub them with garlic.

ACQUACOTTA

Ingredients

olive oil 4-5 tbsp
ripe tomatoes 400-500 g
bread 8 fette
salt, pepper
onions 3-4
eggs 4
garlic

Preparation

In a large saucepan, cook the finely chopped onions over low heat. Soon add the chopped tomatoes.

Continue to cook over moderate heat, stirring frequently. Pour some warm water to dilute the mixture to the consistency of a broth. Add salt and pepper. Continue to cook for half an hour.

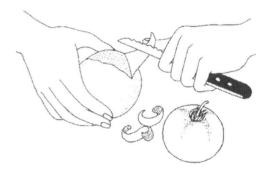

Just before serving, place the eggs, one by one, in the acquacotta. As soon as the egg white has coagulated, catch the eggs with a spoon and place them on each slice of the toasted bread, already rubbed with garlic, in the serving bowls, accompanying them with a portion of acquacotta.

Optional ingredients: ricotta cheese, prosciutto, red bell peppers, celery, mushrooms, basil, zucchini, sausages, peperoncino, parsley, rosemary, broad beans, onions, dried bacon, lard, tomato paste, chard, sausages, pasta (to be boiled in the acquacotta), and in the end - grated cheese.

CARCERATO
PRISONER SOUP

This dish, one of the typical dishes of the traditional Pistoia cuisine, in fact is a soup that is obtained by cooking yesterday's bread in the broth of the veal entrails, to which, today, vegetables are added, such as onions, carrots, celery, tomatoes and in the end some grated cheese with pepper.

Tradition has it that the name of this dish derives from the Pistoia prison of Santa Caterina in which it was prepared using the scraps of nearby municipal slaughterhouses.

CIPOLLATA

La cipollata is a sort of an onion soup cooked with pork meat, fresh or cured.

CIPOLLATA
WITH CURED MEAT
(con pancetta e prosciutto crudo)

Peel and slice the onions (1 kg). Cut the pancetta and prosciutto ham to pieces, not too small.

Peel the carrot and grate it. Chop the celery leaves.

In a pot, boil the cured meat with celery and carrot.

In another pot, gently fry the pancetta and onions in olive oil, over low heat, for 15-20 minutes.

Then pour two or three ladles of the cured meat broth and continue coo-

king for another 15-20 minutes. After that add the pieces of the meat and pour 2-3 ladles of the broth. Continue cooking over low heat for another 30-45 minutes, adding a little broth or water occasionally.

Serve the soup over the slices of bread, rustic, toasted and rubbed with garlic. You can sprinkle with some fresh tasty olive oil.

Optional ingredients: sausages, and in the end grated cheese or eggs.

Optional proceeding: Leave the sliced onions overnight, to soak in water.

CIPOLLATA
WITH PORK MEAT
(con carne di maiale)

In a pot with the vegetable broth (or in the water seasoned with the powdered vegetable broth), 1 liter, cook the fresh pork, 0.7-1 kg, with the bone. Additional herbs may be added, like celery, carrots, parsley or garlic.

About 1.5-2 hours later, remove the bones off the meat and cut the meat into small pieces. Put the meat back in the broth.

Peel and slice the onions. In another

pot, gently fry chopped onions (0,5-1 kg) in olive oil, over low heat, for 5-6 minutes. Then pour two or three ladles of the broth and stir in the flour (1-2 tablespoons).

Continue cooking the onions for another 10-15 minutes. Then add the broth with the meat and continue cooking for 30-45 minutes more. Season with salt and pepper.

Serve the thick soup, over toasted slices of bread.

CARABACCIA
ONION SOUP

Ingredients

red onions 1 kg
fresh sheep cheese 100 g
dry white wine 50-60 ml
toasted bread slices 8
broad beans 50 g
olive oil 4-5 tbsp
salt, pepper
carrots 1-2
peas 100 g
celery
basil

Preparation

Peel and finely slice the onions. Chop the carrot, celery and basil.

Lightly fry the carrot, celery and basil in a pot in oil. Pour the onion and let it fry over low heat. From time to time add a little wine and later some water or vegetable broth.

Then add the peas and broad beans. Stir a few times and pour a liter of broth or water.

Continue cooking for another 30-45 minutes.

Remove the pot from the heat and pour the cheese. Stir and after that season with salt and pepper.

Serve this Florentine onion soup in bowls over slices of toasted bread.

Optional ingredients: grated pecorino, Parmesan cheese, grana padano or gruyere, instead of fresh pecorino, sugar, garlic, cinnamon, almonds, lard.

Optional additions at the end: grated cheese, egg.

Optional omissions: broad beans.

CAVOLATA
INCAVOLATA TOSCANA
FARINATA DI CAVOLO NERO

Ingredients

tuscan kale (cavolo nero) 300-500 g
sheep cheese (pecorino) 50-70 g
borlotti (or toscanelli) beans
(fresh or frozen)
500-600 g
vegetable bouillon powder
fresh tomatoes 1-3
or
tomato paste 1-2 tbsp
corn flour 150-300 g
olive oil 4-5 tbsp
garlic 1-2 cloves
lard 50-100 g
salt, pepper
onion 1
sage

Preparation

In a pot pour some oil and add the chopped lard, onion, garlic and sage. Fry them gently, not long, and then pour in more than 1 litre of water.

When the water starts boiling add the beans, chopped tomatoes, and vegetable bouillon powder or cube. Cook for 10-20 minutes over medium heat, until the beans are cooked. Then crush half of the cooked beans. After that throw in the tuscan kale, soft parts, cut into short and narrow strips. Broccoli, leaf cabbage or couliflower also may be added. Continue cooking for a 10-15 minutes and then pour in the corn flour, gradually. Cook as long as it takes for the kale to be properly cooked. Before the end, soup pasta may be added. In the end season with fresh olive oil, salt and pepper and stir in the grated sheep cheese.

Notes: Farinata di cavalo nero, or farinata con le leghe, is a typical dish of Pistoia. But on the Tuscan coast it is known as bordatino.

Optional ingredients: carrots, celery, leeks, thyme.

ZUPPA DI CECI
E FUNGHI PORCINI
CHICKPEA AND PORCINI
MUSHROOMS
SOUP

Ingredients

well boiled chickpeas 300-500 g
young porcini mushrooms 300-500 g
dry red wine 200-300 ml
olive oil 4-5 tbsp
garlic 1-3 cloves
tomatoes 4-5
salt, pepper
marjoram
onion 1
parsley
celery

Preparation

In a pot gently fry the finely chopped garlic, onion, parsley and celery. Then add the porcini mushrooms cut into thin slices and the boiled chickpeas. Keep on cooking over medium heat for a few minutes, stirring often. Season with salt and then add the white wine. Let it almost evaporate. Pour in some water, or even better, some meat broth. Add the chopped peeled tomatoes. Boil for a quarter of an hour. Season with fresh ground pepper. Serve in rustic bowls or soup bowls garnished with slices of toasted bread. Add some fresh olive oil and the leaves of the fresh marjoram.

CALDARO

CALDARO DELL'ARGENTARIO
FISH AND SEAFOOD STEW

Ingredients

assorted white fish 1 kg
shellfish (mussels or other) 500 g
scampi or shrimp 200-300 g
dry white wine 100 ml
tomatoes 1-5
or
tomato paste 1-3 tbsp
olive oil 4-5 tbsp
garlic 1-2 cloves
small octopus 1
bread slices 4-8
potatoes 3-4
peperoncino
cuttlefish 1
squid 1-2
onion 1
parsley
salt

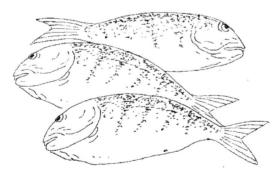

Preparation

Thoroughly clean the fish. Cut the cut-tlefish into small strips. Cut the octopus into small pieces. Peel and cut the potatoes and tomatoes. Finally chop the onion and parsley. Peel and then crush the garlic cloves.

In a pot warm up some olive oil. Gently fry the onion. Add the parsley and garlic, stir a few times, and then add the tomatoes and potatoes. Cook about 10 minutes. If necessary, pour in some water or fish broth.

Put the fish and the seafood and into the same pot. Cook 15-20 minutes. If necessary pour some water or fish broth from time to time.

Serve the fish and the seafood over the (toasted and then aromatized with garlic and olive oil) bread slices (not obligatory).

Note: This dish is especially popular in the Argentario part of Tuscany coast.

Its name comes from a (large) pot type, traditionally used in preparing the dish, called the same - "caldaro".

The dish is similar to "caciucco", also a "zuppa di pesce" but usually it is not that much dense.

ZUPPA ARCIDOSSINA

Ingredients

(sheep) ricotta cheese 300-500 g
vegetable bouillon powder or stock
peeled tomatoes 300-500 g
peperoncino (chili pepper)
spinach 500-800 g
olive oil 3-5 tbsp
bread slices 4-8
onions 2-4
celery
salt

Preparation

Wash, squeeze and then chop the spinach. In a pan, fry the thinly chopped onions in olive oil. Add the spinach. Season with the chilli pepper, salt, pepper and nutmeg. A few minutes later add the chopped tomatoes, vegetable stock and crumbled ricotta. Cook for another 15-20 minutes until all the ingredients are well cooked.

Serve the soup over toasted bread slices.

Optional ingredients: red wine, nutmeg.

Note: The arcidossina soup belongs to the rural kitchen of the farms and villages located on the slopes of Mount Amiata, in Tuscany.

PANZANELLA

Ingredients

one or two days old bread 300-500 g
white vinegar 3-5 tbsp
tomatoes 200-300 g
olive oil 3-5 tbsp
cucumber 1
salt, pepper
onion 1
basil

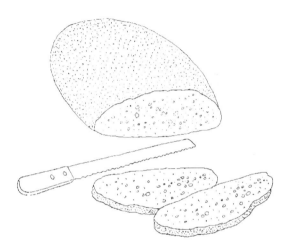

Preparation

Cut the bread into slices about 1 cm thick and then into cubes. Put the cubes in a bowl. Pour in a glass or two of water. In the end the soaked bread should not be too wet. Stir carefully. Let the bread soak for 40-45 minutes.

Peel the onion, cut it into thin slices and let it marinate in vinegar and water, in another bowl, for at least a half an hour. After that, drain the onion slices.

Peel the cucumber, cut it in half lengthwise, then slice it very thinly.

Peel and then cut the tomatoes into small cubes.

If the soaked bread appears to be too wet, lightly squeeze it.

Add the drained onions and then carefully mix in the tomato cubes, cucumber slices and chopped basil.

Then season the salad with olive oil, vinegar, pepper and salt.

Let the salad, the panzanella, rest in the refrigerator for about 1 hour. Remove it 10-15 minutes before serving.

Optional ingredients: boiled eggs, salted enchovies, canned tuna, celery, parsley, green or red chicory, capers, bell peppers, mozzarella other type of (soft) cheese, frankfurters.

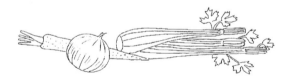

Note: In Lamoli, a small fraction of the Municipality of Borgo Pace, neighbouring the Tuscan region, every summer the Festival of panzanella is organised, ever since 1968.

LA ZUPPA LOMBARDA

Ingredients

a day or two old bread 300-500 g

small white beans (cannellini) 250-300 g
olive oil 4-5 tbsp
salt, pepper

Preparation

Boil the soaked beans in some water, not too much. At the end, remove the pan and transfer the beans into a bowl. Add the toasted bread, cut into small cubes before toasting in a pan, and season with the olive oil, salt and pepper.

Optional ingredients: garlic, vinegar, sage, parsley, thyme, graated (sheep) cheese, chopped peeled tomatoes.

Note: The soup was given this a bit confusing name because more than a hundred years ago a colony of Lombard workers moved to Florence region for the railroad construction works. The Tuscans often used to prepare this soup for them. So, the right name of the soup in fact should be "the soup for the Lombards".

PANCOTTO

Ingredients

a day or two old bread 400-500 g
grated (sheep) cheese 70-120 g
olive oil 4-5 tbsp
garlic 1-3 cloves
fresh eggs 2
salt, pepper

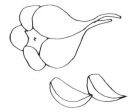

Preparation

In a large and deep saucepan gently fry in olive oil the finely chopped garlic. Then pour in a glass or two of water, and season with salt and pepper.

As soon as the water boils, add the bread cut into pieces and cook for a couple of minutes.

After that, remove the pan from the heat and, after a minute or two, season with grated pecorino and the two eggs. Stir, mixing it all well. Serve with a drizzle of olive oil.

Optional ingredients: chopped sausages, diced bacon, zucchini, ripe tomatoes, peperoncino, onion, parsley, basil, marjoram, meat cube, vegetable bouillon powder or cube, carrot, celery, potatoes, nepetella (mentuccia).

Notes: The quality of the bread used is fundamental.

It is important not to serve the pancotto immediately after it is cooked. Serve it after a ten minute rest.

GARMUGIA

Ingredients

ground or diced veal meat 150-200 g
vegetable bouillon powder or cube
or
meat cube
diced toasted bread slices 4-8
pancetta (bacon) 100-150 g
broad beans 250-400 g
asparagus 150-200 g
lemon juice 1-2 tsp
spring onions 4-7
olive oil 4-5 tbsp
peas 150-300 g
artichokes 3-4
salt, pepper

Preparation

Slice the artichokes finely and chop the onions and asparagus. Dice the pancetta. Chop coarsely the broad beans.

In a deep casserole in olive oil gently fry the onions and the diced pancetta.

When the onion becomes translucent add the ground or diced veal meat and brown it, stirring frequently.

Then add the peas, broad beans, artichokes and asparagus. Season with salt and pepper. Pour in the lemon juice. Stir in some vegetable bouillon powder or a vegetable or a meat cube. Cook over moderate heat.

Continue cooking, stirring occasionally. Pour in some water or broth from time to time, but only if it is really necessary. Cook over moderate heat, for 30-40 minutes. Serve with diced toasted bread.

Note: Garmugia, also known as gramugia, is a soup that originated in Lucca, Tuscany.

Optional additions: raw ham (instead of pancetta), lard, sausage, pecorino, carrot, onions instead of spring onions.

GINESTRATA

Ingredients

chicken soup 500 ml or chichen stock
dry vin santo or marsala wine 4 tbsp
cinnamon ½ tsp
sugar ½ tsp
butter 60 g
nutmeg
uova 4

Preparation

Beat the egg whites until they become stiff.

Beat the egg yolks with a spoon of sugar.

In a pot join the whites to the yolks, adding the vin santo, cinnamon and, gradually, the broth.

Put the mixture on the fire, Add the butter, stirring often.

When the cream has thickened, remove it from the heat, pour it into the soup plates and cover the surface with the sugar and a pinch of nutmeg.

It is possible to put the mixture in the oven for a few minutes. Eventually it will resemble a pudding.

Optional ingredients

Chiodi di garofano, coriandolo, Madeira wine

Optional proceeding

Ginestrata may be strained using a sieve.

Note

Ginestrata, a soup that is originated in Tuscany, can be described as a thin, lightly spiced egg-based soup.

PASTA

PASTA TOSCANA

Although today the assortment of the pasta types used for preparing pasta dishes in Tuscany is very wide, due to a versatile supply in the supermarkets, some pasta formats are still considered as substantially Tuscan.

PICI

The most recognizable Tuscan pasta type is the famous "pici" (pronounced "peachi").

It is a thick type of pasta, similar to spaghettoni. Traditionally pici are home-made and hand-rolled.

Pici originate in the province of Siena in Tuscany. In the Montalcino area they are called pinci.

The pici dough is typically made only from flour and water. The addition of eggs is optional. Finely chopped spinach can also be added.

The dough is rolled out in a thick flat sheet which is then cut into strips.

The home-made pici are not uniform in size and have variations of thickness along its length.

The boiled pici can be seasoned with various types of sauces like the aglione sauce (garlic and tomatoes), briciole (breadcrumbs) sauce, mushrooms, cacio e pepe (cheese and pepper) and meat-based sauces (wild boar, hare or duck).

Pici (pinci), pici senesi, is a typical pasta format from southern Tuscany, but also from Umbria (called umbricelli, lombrichelli or stringoli).

PICI ALL'AGLIONE

Ingredients

pici type pasta 400 g
peperoncino (chilli pepper)

dry white wine 100 ml
tomatoes 500-800 g
olive oil 4-5 tbsp
garlic 3-6 cloves
salt

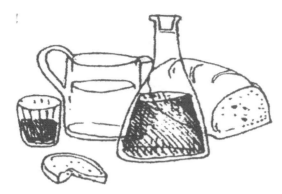

The aglione variety of garlic differs from the other types of garlic for a specific delicate, somewhat sweet taste. The weight of this garlic variety may reach up to 800 g.

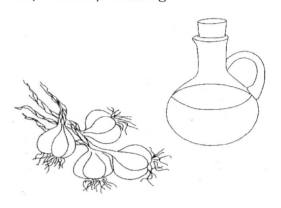

Preparation

Peel the tomatoes and cut them into small pieces. Peel and crush the garlic cloves. Chop finely the chilli pepper.

In a saucepan, lightly fry the garlic, on oil, over a very low heat. Then add the tomatoes, chilli pepper and wine. Continue cooking over low heat for 20 minutes. Season with salt and then remove the sauce from the heat.

Meanwhile cook the pasta in abundant salted water. Drain the pasta al dente and stir it in the saucepan with the sauce. Briefly warm up over moderate heat (optional), and then serve the hot pici, with grated cheese.

Optional ingredients: spaghettoni instead of pici, pepper instead of chilli, aglio instead of aglione, dried chilli instead of fresh, sugar, tomato sauce instead of fresh or peeled tomatoes, white vinegar, carrots, onions, celery.

Possible omissions: peperoncino.

Note: Pici all'aglione is a traditional dish of the Val di Chiana, one of the most fertile lands in Tuscany. This dish is based on a typical local product - the Chiana aglione.

PICI ALL'ESTRUSCA

Mince and mix the hard-boiled egg with the garlic cloves, parsley, mint and basil. Pour in some olive oil in a way to obtain a rather fluid sauce. Season with salt and pepper.

Season the boiled pici with the prepared sauce, sprinkle with grated pecorino and serve.

PICI
ALLE BRICIOLE
PICI WITH BREADCRUMBS

Ingredients

pici type pasta 400 g
peperoncino (chilli pepper)
one or two days old bread,
without crust
100-150 g
olive oil 3-5 tbsp
garlic 2-3 cloves

Preparation

Cut the bread into pieces. Blend them using a mixer.

In a saucepan warm up the oil and gently fry the crushed garlic. Add the peperoncino, stir and then put in the blended bread. Stir again, and soon remove the pan from the heat.

Meanwhile cook the pasta in abundant salted water.

Drain the pasta al dente and stir it in the saucepan with the sauce. Mix everything, briefly warm up over moderate heat, pouring in some liquid remaining from boiling the pasta, if necessary, and then serve the hot pici, accompanied by some grated sheep cheese.

Optional ingredients of the sauce: minced salted enchovies, diced pancetta (bacon), pepper instead of peperoncino, chopped (fresh) sausage, leeks, zucchini, and in the end - ricotta cheese or cherry tomatoes.

In a saucepan gently fry in oil the prepared seasonings - carrot, celery and onion. Then add the meat and fry untill it turns brown. Pour in the wine and let it almost evaporate. Then add the diced tomatoes. Season with salt and pepper. Continue cooking for a couple of hours over moderate heat.

Meanwhile cook the pasta in abundant salted water. Drain the pasta al dente and stir it in the saucepan with the sauce.

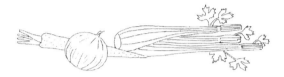

Optional ingredients: rabbit meat instead of viel and pork meat, truffles or other types of mushrooms.

Note: The chianina meat gives a special flavor to the sauce. The Chianina is a famous Italian breed of cattle.

PICI
AL RAGÙ TOSCANO
PICI WITH TUSCAN MEAT SAUCE

Ingredients

pici type pasta 400 g
canned peeled tomatoes 700-800 g
fresh tomatoes 0,8-1kg
or
tomato passata 500-700 g
ground pork meat 150-250 g
ground viel meat 400-500 g
red wine 100-200 ml
olive oil 4-5 tbsp
salt, pepper
rosemary
carrot 1
onion 1
celery

Preparation

PICI
AI FAGIOLI
PICI WITH BEANS

Ingredients

pici type pasta 400 g
small white cannellini beans
(fresh or frozen)
350-500 g
tomato passata 500-700 g
or
fresh tomatoes 0,8-1kg
olive oil 4-5 tbsp
garlic 1-3 cloves
salt, pepper

Preparation

In a saucepan gently fry in olive oil the crushed garlic. Then add the beans and the tomatoes. Season with salt and pepper. Continue cooking until the beans and the sauce are ready.

Meanwhile cook the pasta in abundant salted water.

Drain the pasta al dente and stir it in the saucepan with the sauce. Season with grated cheese and some chopped basil or thyme.

PICI CACIO E PEPE

CHEESE AND PEPPER PICI

Ingredients

pici type pasta 400 g
coarsely grated pecorino cheese 150-300 g
black pepper
salt

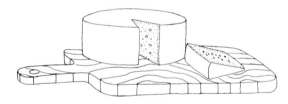

Preparation

Cook the pasta in an abundant quantity of salted water.

Drain the boiled pasta "al dente", season it with the sauce and serve it promptly.

Season the pasta with grated hard cheese (use some sheep cheese or/and cow cheese) and pepper, ground at the moment.

If necessary add some liquid which you have saved after cooking and draining the pasta.

Note: Instead of black pepper, the white, red or green pepper may used.

Optional ingredients: minced nuts, ricotta.

Do not season the drained pasta in the warm pot or a saucepan, to avoid melting of the cheese.

PICI AL FUMO

SMOKED PICI

Ingredients

pici type pasta
(or spaghetti, bucatini or penne) 400 g
smoked pancetta (bacon) 150-250 g
fresh peperoncino (chilli pepper) 1-3
concentrated tomato paste 1-3 tbsp
cooking cream 100 ml
vodka 1 little glass
olive oil 4-5 tbsp
garlic 1-3 cloves
rosemary

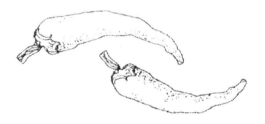

Preparation

In a saucepan gently fry in olive oil the diced and minced bacon, garlic, cloves cut in halves and squashed, chopped chilli peppers and rosemary leaves, still on little branches.

After a couple of minutes of constant stirring, remove the garlic and the rosemary. Then pour and stir in a small dose of vodka. After that, add the tomato paste and cook for 4-5 minutes. Then stir in the cream and cook for a minute more. No, or very little salt should be added.

Cook the pasta in an abundant quantity of salted water.

Drain the boiled pasta "al dente", transfer it into the saucepan with the sauce and stir gently over a moderate heat, not more than a minute or two.

Note: This dish is a specialty of Cortona.

PICI
AI FUNGHI

PICI WITH MUSHROOMS

Ingredients

pici type pasta
(or pappardelle, penne, fusilli)
400 g
mushrooms
(porcini, truffles, champignon)
300-800 g
cooking cream 100-250 ml
olive oil 3-4 tbsp
salt

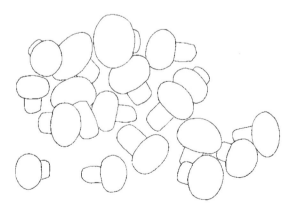

Preparation

Clean the mushrooms and slice them thinly.

Braise the mushrooms with some oil, over moderate heat, stirring often.

Let most of the liquid evaporate. After that remove the mushrooms from the heat.

Cook the pasta in an abundant quantity of salted water.

Drain the pasta "al dente" (firm to the bite), mix it with the mushroom sauce, joining also the cream, and serve it immediately.

Optional ingredients: milk instead of cream, tomatoes, black or green olives, (minced) meat, yellow bell peppers, leeks, peas, chicken livers, zucchini, canned tuna, artichokes, scampi o shrimp tails, dried mushrooms, pancetta (dried bacon), ricotta cheese, robiola, truffles, black olives, thyme.

Optional herbs and spices: pepper, garlic, onions, parsley, cognac, chili peppers, vegetable powder bouillon, shallots, green onions, white bulb onions, sausages, carrots, mint, thyme, eggs, egg yolks, cooked eggs, tomatoes, cherry tomatoes, oregano, celery, paprika powder, bechamel sauce, bay leaves, sage, cheese, chives, capers, marjoram, basil, sugar, rosemary, rocket salad, nutmeg, red or white wine, sweet wine, lemon zest and juice, pine nuts, vinegar, sour cream, desalted anchovy fillets, bread crumbs, mustard.

Optional ingredients at the end: grated cheese.

Possible omissions: cream.

Different name for the dish: pici alla boscaiola.

PAPPARDELLE

Besides pici, pappardelle also represent well the best of the Tuscan pasta selection.

The term "pappardelle" derives from the Latin verb "pappare", i.e. to eat, which in the Tuscan dialect corresponds to consuming a food with joy and pleasure.

Today pappardelle is a typical Tuscan pasta type, made of a mixture of flour, eggs and salt, to form the wide and rough on the surface strips.

This egg pasta, very similar to the tagliatelle in the shape, is characterized by a greater width: while the tagliatelle are from 4 to 10 millimeters wide, the pappardelle can vary from 2 to 3 cm. This measure makes them recognizable compared to other similar egg pasta such as fettuccine (3-5 mm wide) or tagliolini (about 2 mm).

The search for the origin of this pasta leads right to Tuscany. Although the pappardelle are widespread in central and northern Italy, they are considerably more used in Tuscan cuisine, where they are combined with full-bodied sauces, above all those based on game or mushrooms. Among the sauces typically used, perhaps the most famous is the wild boar meat sauce.

PAPPARDELLE AL CINGHIALE
PAPPARDELLE WITH WILD BOAR RAGÙ

Ingredients

pasta
(pappardelle,
or
tagliatelle, fettuccine or pici)
400 g
wild boar meat
(cut in pieces or ground)
500-800 g
fresh tomatoes 500-600 g
or

tomato passata 500-700 g
red wine 50-100 ml
olive oil 4-5 tbsp
garlic 1-2 cloves
juniper berries
salt, pepper
bay leaves
rosemary
onion 1-2
carrot 1
celery

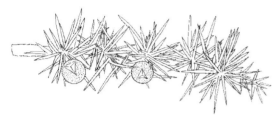

Preparation

In a pot, gently fry the chopped onions, crushed garlic, minced celery and grated carrots, in olive oil, over moderate heat. Then put in the meat and pour in the wine. Let the wine almost evaporate before adding the tomatoes. Season with rosemary, bay leaves, juniper berries, salt and pepper.

Cook for 2, maybe even for 3 hours, over a moderate heat, until the meat is quite tender.

Boil the pasta in an abundant quantity of salted water.

Drain the pasta al dente and stir it in the saucepan with the sauce. Mix everything, briefly warming the pasta over moderate heat, pouring in some liquid remaining from boiling the pasta, if necessary, and then serve the hot pappardelle, accompanied by some grated sheep cheese.

Optional ingredients: pancetta (bacon), parsley, sausages, cloves, sage, cognac, cooking cream, vegetable or meat bouillon powder or cube.

Optional, but advisable proceeding: Transfer the wild boar meat into a bowl. Add some red wine, a grated carrot, chopped onions, pepper, rosemary and juniper berries. Let the meat marinate overnight. After that, drain the meat and cut it to pieces.

Do not use the ingredients of the marinade in the further course of the preparation of the dish. Use fresh seasonings, onions and other.

Note: Pappardelle with wild boar ragù are one of the most popular first courses of Tuscan cuisine and Maremma cuisine in particular.

PAPPARDELLE AL CINGHIALE IN BIANCO

PAPPARDELLE WITH WILD BOAR RAGÙ IN WHITE

Ingredients

pasta
(pappardelle,
or
tagliatelle, fettuccine or pici)
400 g
wild boar meat
(cut in pieces or ground)
500-800 g
sliced (various) mushrooms
150-200 g
diced pancetta (bacon)
80-120 g

olive oil 4-5 tbsp
milk 200-300 ml
garlic 1-2 cloves
juniper berries
salt, pepper
bay leaves
cloves 3-5
cinnamon
rosemary
onion 1-2
carrot 1
celery

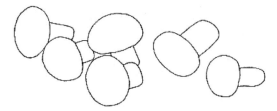

Preparation

In a pot, gently fry the diced bacon. A minute later add the chopped onions, crushed garlic, minced celery and grated carrots, in olive oil, over moderate heat. Then put in the meat and fry for a minute or two, stirring often. Then add the mushrooms. Let the mushrooms release their liquid, while cooking for another 10 minutes. After that, pour in the milk. Season with rosemary, bay leaves, juniper berries, cinnamon, crushed cloves, salt and pepper.

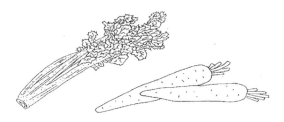

Cook for two, maybe even for three hours, over a moderate, even low heat, until the meat is quite tender.

If and when it is necessary, pour in some water and stir the ingredients.

In the end, remove the saucepan from the heat.

Boil the pasta in an abundant quantity of salted water.

Drain the pasta al dente and stir it in the saucepan with the sauce.

Optional ingredients: cooking cream, dried mushrooms.

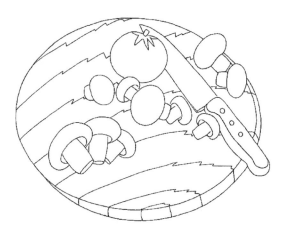

Optional, but advisable proceeding: Transfer the wild boar meat in a bowl. Add some red wine, a grated carrot, chopped onions, pepper, rosemary and juniper berries. Let the meat marinate overnight. After that, drain the meat and cut it to pieces. Do not use the ingredients of the marinade in the further course of the preparation of the dish. Use fresh seasonings, onions and other.

PAPPARDELLE AL SUGO DI LEPRE

PAPPARDELLE WITH HARE RAGÙ

Ingredients

pasta

(pappardelle,
or
tagliatelle, fettuccine or pici)
400 g
hare meat 500-800 g
fresh tomatoes 100-300 g
or
tomato passata 50-200 g
white or red wine
100-150 ml
olive oil 4-5 tbsp
garlic 1-2 cloves
juniper berries
salt, pepper
bay leaves
cloves 3-5
rosemary
onion 1-2
carrot 1
celery

Preparation

In a pot, gently fry the chopped onions, crushed garlic, minced celery and grated carrots, in olive oil, over moderate heat. Then put in the hare meat, already cut to pieces, stir for a minute or two and after that pour in the wine. Let the wine almost evaporate before adding the tomatoes. Season with rosemary, bay leaves, juniper berries, cloves, salt and pepper.

Cook for 1-2 hours, over a moderate heat, until the meat is tender.

Boil the pasta in an abundant quantity of salted water.

Drain the pasta al dente and stir it in the saucepan with the sauce. Mix everything, briefly warming the pasta over moderate heat, pouring in some liquid remaining from boiling the pasta, if necessary, and then serve the hot pappardelle, accompanied by some grated sheep cheese.

Optional ingredients: basil, cooking cream, parsley, peperoncino (chilli peppers), vegetable bouillon powder or cube, meat broth cube.
Optional, but advisable proceeding:

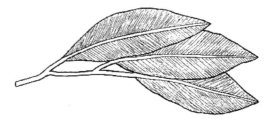

Transfer the hare meat in a bowl. Add some wine, vinegar, a grated carrot, chopped onions, pepper, rosemary and juniper berries. Let the meat marinate overnight. After that, drain the meat and cut it to pieces. Do not use the ingredients of the marinade in the further course of the preparation of the dish. Use fresh seasonings, onions and other.

PAPPARDELLE
AL RAGÙ BIANCO
DI CINTA SENESE

PAPPARDELLE
WITH WHITE RAGÙ
OF THE CINTA SENESE

Ingredients

pasta
(pappardelle,
or
tagliatelle, fettuccine or pici)
400 g
ground cinta senese pork meat
0.8-1 kg

dry white wine 50-100 ml
meat broth 200-300 ml
olive oil 4-5 tbsp
juniper berries
bay leaves 1-3
salt, pepper
carrot 1
onion 1
celery

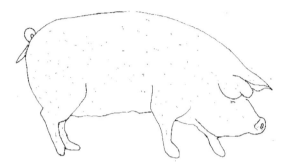

Preparation

In a pot, gently fry the chopped onions, minced celery and grated carrots, in olive oil, over moderate heat. Then put in the pork meat, already cut to pieces, stir for a minute or two and after that pour in the wine. Let the wine almost evaporate before starting to add the meat broth. Season with rosemary, bay leaves, juniper berries, salt and pepper.

Cook for 1-2 hours, over a moderate heat, until the meat is tender.

Boil the pasta in an abundant quantity of salted water.

Drain the pasta al dente and stir it in the saucepan with the sauce. Mix everything, briefly warming the seasoned pasta over moderate heat, pouring in some liquid remaining from boiling the pasta, if necessary, and then serve the hot pappardelle, accompanied by some grated sheep cheese.

Optional ingredients: tomatoes, ro-

semary, cooking cream, parsley, peperoncino (chilli peppers), vegetable bouillon powder or cube, meat broth cube.

Note: The Cinta Senese pig is an ancient breed particularly widespread in the hills of Siena where it is raised in the wild. This gives the explanation of the peculiarity of the intense taste of the cinta senese meat.

PAPPARDELLE ALL'ANATRA
PAPPARDELLE WITH DUCK MEAT RAGÙ

Ingredients

pasta
(pappardelle,
or
tagliatelle, fettuccine or pici)
400 g
little duck (nana, anatra) meat
0.8-1 kg
concentrated tomato paste
1-3 tbsp
dry white wine 150-200 ml
olive oil 4-5 tbsp
salt, pepper
marjoram
carrot 1
onion 1
parsley
thyme
celery

Preparation

In a saucepan, heat two tablespoons

of oil and brown the duck, cut to pieces, over a high heat. Add salt and pepper, cover and continue cooking over a low heat. Remove the meat from the heat.

In a pot, gently fry the chopped onions, minced celery, marjoram, thyme and parsley, and the grated carrots, in olive oil, over moderate heat.

After that put in the duck meat, stir for a minute or two and after that pour in the wine. Let the wine almost evaporate.

Stir in the concentrated tomato paste and season with salt and pepper.

Cook for 1-2 hours, over a moderate heat, until the meat is tender.

Boil the pasta in an abundant quantity of salted water.

Drain the pasta al dente and stir it in the saucepan with the sauce.

Serve the hot pappardelle, accompanied by some grated sheep cheese.

Optional ingredients: duck liver, goose instead of duck meat (pasta all'ocio), sage, basil, prosciutto, pancetta (bacon), fresh tomatoes, vegetable bouillon powder or cube, meat broth cube, noce moscata.

PASTA AL SUGO SCAPPATO
PASTA WITH A NO MEAT SAUCE

Season the pasta (preferably a short pasta type like penne or fusilli) with a sauce prepared frying and cooking onions, celery, carrots, garlic, parsley, basil, white or red wine and tomatoes (the usual sesonings of a meat sauce, but no meat is used in the preparation of this sauce).

Pancetta (bacon) can be added.

Different names of the dish: pasta al sugo falso, pasta al finto sugo, pasta al sugo alla povera.

PAPPARDELLE AI TARTUFI
PAPPARDELLE WITH TRUFFLE MUSHROOMS

Ingredients

pasta
(pappardelle,
or
tagliatelle, fettuccine or pici)
400 g
black or white truffles 70-100 g
olive oil 3-4 tbsp
garlic 1-2 cloves
butter 3-4 tbsp
salt, pepper

Preparation

Rinse the truffles carefully under the tap water. Brush it with a semi-hard brush to remove all traces of impurities. Make sure you clean it well from any traces of soil. Dry the truffles carefully before slicing it.

Slice thinly the truffles, with the special truffle cutter or otherwise.

In a saucepan warm up the oil together with the butter, over low heat.

Peel the garlic clove, cut it in two or three pieces, squeeze them, and let them gently fry in oil and melted butter for a few minutes. Then either leave the garlic in or remove it with a fork. Turn off the heat and add the sliced truffle shavings, stirring a few times. Season with salt and pepper.

Boil the pasta in an abundant quantity of salted water. Drain the pasta al dente and stir it in the saucepan with the sauce.

Optional ingredients: cooking cream, and in the end - grated cheese.

Note: The truffle is an underground mushroom, very delicate.

Truffles are much more attainable in Tuscany than they are in other parts of Italy, or other parts of the world, because they are native to this region.

Truffles have to be searched for in woods using dogs or pigs to detect the scent of the truffles hidden in the ground.

Truffles can be stored in a cool place only for a short period (maximum 7-8 days), wrapped in breathable gauze and closed in a glass jar.

In San Miniato, each year a festival is organized to promote the truffle culinary experiences (Sagra del tartufo bianco).

SPAGHETTI AGLIO, OLIO E PEPERONCINO

SPAGHETTI, GARLIC, OIL AND CHILI PEPPERS

Ingredients

pasta (spaghetti or capellini) 400 g
peperoncino (chili peppers) 1-2
bread crumbs 1-3 tbsp
olive oil 4-5 tbsp
garlic 2-3 cloves
salt

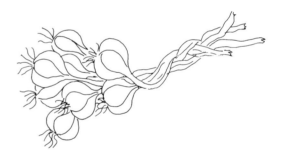

Preparation

Mince the garlic and chili peppers.

In a saucepan warm up the oil and add the garlic and chili peppers. Stir for a minute, over low heat, and then remove the saucepan.

In the meantime, cook the pasta in an abundant quantity of salted water.

Drain the pasta "al dente", season it with the sauce and serve it promptly.

Optional ingredients: salted anchovies, parsley, basil, tomato paste, breadcrumbs, and in the end: minced rocket salad.

Possible omissions: garlic.

Different method: Season the pasta, cooked and drained, with the oil aromatized with garlic and chili peppers (left in the oil for 2-6 hours and removed before use).

Note: Typical dish of the Tuscan cuisine.

PASTA
AL PESTO

PASTA
WITH BASIL AND PINE NUT PESTO

Ingredients

pasta (penne, fusilli, spaghetti) 400 g
grated parmigiano reggiano
or grana padano cheese
6 tbsp
grated pecorino romano, toscano,
sardo or siciliano cheese
2 tbsp
olive oil 4-5 tbsp
basil leaves 50 g
pine nuts 1 tbsp
(coarse) sea salt
garlic 1-3 cloves

Preparation

Grind the garlic and the salt in a mortar. Then add the basil (not all at once), using circular motions.

Later on, add the pine kernels and the cheese. Grind and mix everything well. Then pour in the oil, little by little, blending it in.

Cook the pasta in an abundant quantity of salted water. Drain the pasta "al dente", season it with the sauce (pesto) and serve it.

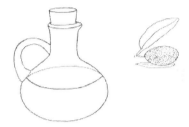

Optional ingredients: walnuts instead of pine kernels.

The best pesto is prepared using a marble mortar and a wooden pestle. The use of a blender or a food processor will give results that can be evaluated only as acceptable, certainly not just as good.

Note: A "pesto" is a mixture of crushed ingredients, prepared primarily in order to season pasta or sometimes minestrone.

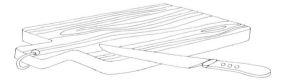

The basil is highly esteemed in the *cucina italiana* as a seasoning. Its name in fact comes from the greek word "basilicon", meaning "*royal* ".

The pine nuts (pine kernels) are the seeds of certain species of pine (Pinus

Pinea - "'umbrella type pine" or other species).

PASTA AL POMODORO

PASTA WITH TOMATO SAUCE

Ingredients

pasta (penne, fusilli, spaghetti) 400 g
ripe (plum) tomatoes 2 kg
olive oil 5-6 tbsp
salt, pepper
sugar 1 tsp
onions 3-5

Preparation

Peel the tomatoes and cut them into small pieces. Peel and chop the onions.

Warm up the oil in a large saucepan and fry gently the onions, over very low heat. Then add the tomatoes. Season with salt and sugar.

Continue cooking the sauce.

In the meantime, cook the pasta in an abundant quantity of salted water.

Drain the pasta "al dente", mix it with the sauce and serve it promptly.

Basic recipe for long-lasting cooking of the tomato sauce

Peel the tomatoes and cut them into small pieces. Finely chop and mince the onions.

In a saucepan fry the onions in oil, over low heat. When the onions start to change its colour, add the tomatoes. Cook for 2-3 hours over low heat. At the end add salt and sugar.

Basic recipe for short-lasting cooking of the tomato sauce

Peel the tomatoes (1-2 lb) and cut them into small pieces. Crush the tomato pieces and let the liquid drain off.

Cook the tomatoes over medium heat for 10-15 minutes letting the tomatoes lose its raw taste. Add the sugar and salt. At the very end of the cooking, possibly blend into the thickened sauce some crushed or finely chopped herbs.

Optional ingredients, herbs and spices: whole canned plum tomatoes instead of fresh tomatoes, tomato paste, basil, carrots, peppers, parsley, garlic, rosemary, vinegar, aceto balsamico, peperoncino chili peppers, celery, capers, pine nuts, desalted anchovy fillets, green or black olives, (ground) almonds, marjoram, dry white wine, lemon juice or lemon peel, vegetable soup powder, nutmeg, cloves, thyme, aubergines, mint, paprika powder, cinnamon, breadcrumbs, mustard, cheese, coriander seeds, raisins, sweet wine, (ground) walnuts, butter, oregano, dried tomatoes, roux (flour cooked with butter), mushrooms, cream, rocket salad, red wine, canned tuna fish, pancetta (dried bacon), olive paste, prunes (dried plums), shallots.

Optional ingredients at the end: chives, grated cheese.

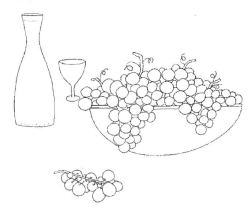

Note: Tomato sauce may be frozen successfully. After thawing, let it simmer for 5-6 minutes, over low heat, before seasoning the pasta.

Warning: Do not put too many different ingredients, herbs and spices into the sauce. Add sparingly, tasting the sauce from time to time, especially when it is already thickened.

PASTA AL POMODORO CRUDO

PASTA WITH RAW TOMATOES

Ingredients

pasta (penne, fusilli, spaghetti) 400 g
tomatoes (ripe but firm)
or
cherry tomatoes 500 g
basil or/and other herbs
garlic 1-3 cloves
salt, pepper
olive oil

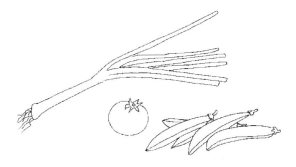

Preparation

Peel the tomatoes, cut them into small pieces and mix them with the crushed or minced garlic. Add chopped herbs (basil and/or other). Pour in some olive oil and season with the salt and pepper.

In the meantime, cook the pasta in an abundant quantity of salted water.

Drain the pasta "al dente", add it into the sauce and serve it promptly.

Optional primary ingredients: bell peppers, canned tuna fish, desalted anchovy fillets, smoked ham, pancetta (dried bacon), rocket salad, shrimp or scampi tails (peeled and briefly cooked), dried tomatoes instead of fresh.

Optional herbs and spices: peperon-cino chili peppers instead of ground pepper, parsley, capers, vinegar, chives, onion, shallots, fennel, coriander, mint, paprika, carrot, nutmeg, pine nuts, black or green olives, cloves, grated cheese, peppers, lemon juice or lemon peel, brandy.

Optional proceeding: A food processor (blender) may be used in the process of preparing the sauce.

PASTA CON SALSA ROSSA

PASTA
WITH RED SAUCE

Ingredients

pasta (penne, fusilli, spaghetti) 400 g
brown or vegetable stock 2 cups
ripe (plum) tomatoes 500 g
paprika powder 1-2 tsp
olive oil 4-5 tbsp
flour 1-2 tsp
sugar 1 tsp
onion 1
salt

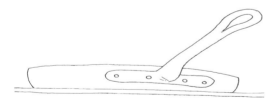

Preparation

Peel the tomatoes and cut them into small pieces. Mince the onion.

Warm up the oil in a saucepan and fry the onion, over low heat. Then put in the tomatoes. Cook for 5-10 minutes over medium heat. After that, pour in the stock and continue cooking for another 10-15 minutes, still over medium heat.

Filter the sauce and then add the flour (already melted in some water). Cook for 5-6 minutes, still over rather low heat. Then sparingly season the sauce with paprika powder, sugar and salt.

Cook the pasta in an abundant quantity of salted water.

Drain the pasta "al dente", add it into the sauce and serve it promptly.

Optional ingredients: red bell peppers, peperoncino chili peppers, garlic, vinegar, sugar, dry white wine, carrot, celery, sage, rosemary, basil, bay leaves, ground pepper.

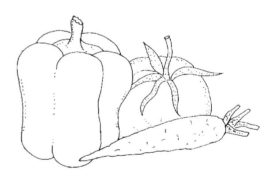

Optional ingredients at the end: cinnamon, mustard, grated cheese.

Note: The stock is a flavoured liquid base for making a sauce.

A *white stock* is prepared by placing the ingredients directly into the water.

In a *brown stock* the ingredients are first browned in fat and then the liquid is added.

Stocks can be used in thickened or unthickened form.

Stocks can be based on vegetables, fish, veal, beef, bones, poultry, game and aromatic herbs and vegetables.

PASTA AL FRIGGIONE

PASTA WITH TOMATO AND BELL PEPPER SAUCE

Ingredients

pasta (penne, fusilli, spaghetti) 400 g
ripe (plum) tomatoes 250-700 g
onions (white) 0,5-2 kg
olive oil 2-3 tbsp
bell peppers 1-3
sugar 0.5-1 tsp
salt

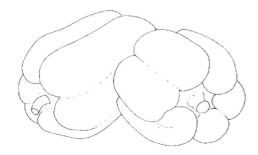

Preparation

Peel the onions and cut them into thin slices. Sprinkle with salt and sugar and leave the onions to macerate for 1-2 hours.

Peel and finely chop the tomatoes. Clean the peppers and cut them in small pieces.

Warm up the oil in a saucepan. Cook slowly the onions, over low heat. Then add the tomatoes and peppers and continue cooking for another hour or even two.

In the meantime, cook the pasta in an abundant quantity of salted water. Drain the pasta "al dente", mix it with the sauce and serve it promptly.

Optional herbs and spices: sugar, chili peppers, garlic, potatoes.

Suggestions: The friggione sauce can also be served over crostini.

PASTA AL POMODORO E MELANZANE

PASTA WITH TOMATO AND EGGPLANT SAUCE

Ingredients

pasta (penne, fusilli, spaghetti) 400 g
yellow or/and red bell peppers 1-2
desalted anchovy fillets 3-5
ripe tomatoes 500-800 g
green olives 1-2 oz
olive oil 4-5 tbsp
garlic 1-3 cloves
capers 1-3 tbsp
eggplants 1-3
salt, pepper
basil

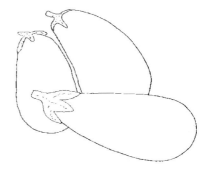

Preparation

Peel the tomatoes and dice them.

Mince the capers and the anchovy fillets. Seed the bell peppers and cut them into short strips. Chop the olives. Mince finely the garlic. Chop the basil.

Peel the eggplants and cut them into small cubes. Sprinkle them with some salt and allow the eggplants to rest for half an hour, or an hour, to loose the bitter juices. Then rinse the eggplants and let them drain off.

Warm up the oil in a pan and briefly fry the garlic, over low heat. Add eggplants and increase the heat. A couple of minutes later, add also the tomatoes and peppers. Continue cooking over moderate heat for another 15-20 minutes. Then put in anchovies, capers, olives, basil, salt and pepper. Let it simmer for a few minutes, turn down the heat and remove the pan.

Cook the pasta in an abundant quantity of salted water.

Drain the pasta "al dente", firm to the bite, mix it with the sauce and serve it immediately.

Optional ingredients: zucchini, onions.

Optional ingredients at the end: ricotta cheese, grated cheese, fried eggplant slices.

BUCATINI AI POMODORI E PANCETTA

PASTA
WITH TOMATO AND BACON
SAUCE

Ingredients

pasta (penne, fusilli, spaghetti) 400 g
pancetta (dried bacon) 100-150 g
tomatoes 250-350 g
grated cheese 50 g
olive oil 2-3 tbsp
salt, pepper
onion 1

Preparation

Dice the pancetta (or bacon) and mince the onion. Peel the tomatoes and cut them into small pieces.

Fry the pancetta for a minute or two, in warm oil, and then add the minced onion. Continue frying over low heat for a couple of minutes. Then put in the tomatoes. Cook over medium heat until the liquid, contained in the tomatoes, evaporates. Season with salt and pepper and add some grated cheese. Stir a couple of times.

Cook the pasta in an abundant quantity of salted water. Drain the pasta "al dente" (firm to the bite), mix it with the sauce and serve.

Optional herbs and spices: peperoncino chili peppers (instead of pepper), dry white whine, basil.

Possible omissions: onions or tomatoes.

Optional proceeding: Fry the diced pancetta separately and add it to the sauce a few moments before removing it from the heat.

PASTA
ALLE ERBE

PASTA WITH HERBS

Ingredients

pasta (penne, fusilli, spaghetti) 400 g
selected aromatic herbs
olive oil 4-5 tbsp
salt

Preparation

Cook the pasta, drain it and then season it with a herb sauce, already prepared by mincing, chopping, crushing, mashing, whipping, whisking and/or beating aromatic herbs with a knife, with a mortar and a pestle, with a blender, with a food processor or with an immersion mixer, possibly subsequently frying the minced herbs, over low heat, adding oil or butter and some salt, and/or, in some instances, blending them with other additional ingredients also.

Herbs

Select one, two or more of the ap-

propriate aromatic herbs: garlic, green onions, onions, basil, parsley, capers, sage, marjoram, chives, rosemary, shallots, bay leaves, thyme, oregano, mint, rocket salad, celery, carrots, chili peppers, pepper, saffron.

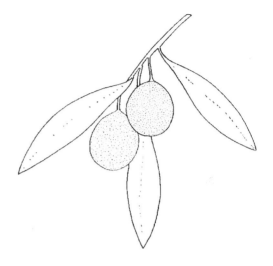

Other ingredients

Tomatoes (raw, paste, passata), cream, green or black olives, dry white wine, red wine, sweet wine, cognac (brandy), vinegar, balsamic vinegar (aceto balsamico), lemon zest and juice, orange zest and juice, concentrated meat, fish, crab or vegetable soup, sour cream, desalted anchovy fillets, egg yolks, cheese, leeks, mayonnaise, pancetta (dried bacon), prosciutto ham, bell peppers, prunes, mushrooms, raisins, almonds, walnuts, cinnamon, paprika powder, pine nuts, sugar, mustard, bread crumbs, pickled gherkins, nutmeg, honey, tabasco sauce, worcestershire sauce, soft inside of a bread slice, milk.

Warning: Do not put too many different herbs and spices into the food. Add the seasonings gradually, tasting the sauce more than once in order to balance the flavours.

Note: By mixing the above mentioned

herbs and ingredients it is possible to achieve thousands of successful combinations. Choose your own favorites.

PASTA ALLE VERDURE

PASTA WITH VEGETABLES

Ingredients

pasta (penne, fusilli, spaghetti) 400 g
pancetta (dried bacon) 50-100 g
green beans 100-150 g
olive oil 4-5 tbsp
peas 100-150 g
salt, pepper
zucchini 1-3
celery 1 rib
onions 1-2
carrot 1
basil

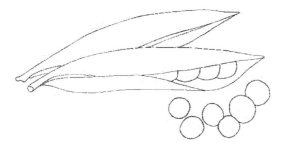

Preparation

Cut the zucchini, green beans and carrot into pieces. Cut the bacon into small cubes. Mince the onions, celery and basil.

In a pan warm up the oil and gently fry the onions, over low heat. A minute or two later, add bacon, carrot and celery. Stir a few times, and then put in peas, zucchini and green beans. Season with salt and pepper.

Continue the cooking for 10-15 minutes over medium heat, stirring often.

After that remove the pan from the heat and add some coarsly chopped basil leaves.

In the meantime, cook the pasta in an abundant quantity of salted water.

Drain the pasta "al dente", firm to the bite, mix it with the sauce and serve it immediately.

Optional primary ingredients: green or red bell peppers, leeks (the white part), artichokes, tomatoes, mushrooms, (fried) eggplants, potatoes, shrimps, ham, asparagus, desalted anchovy fillets, pine nuts, canned tuna, green or black olives, shrimp or scampi tails.

Optional herbs and spices: capers, vegetable powder bouillon, various fresh aromatic herbs, chili powder, dry white wine, cream, garlic, marjoram, oregano, basil, parsley, lemon zest and juice.

Optional ingredients at the end: grated cheese, ricotta cheese, mozzarella.

Optional proceeding: Boil the vegetables or fry them before further use.

Different method: Season the pasta with grilled vegetables (eggplants, zucchini, tomatoes, bell peppers ...).

PASTA ALLA BOSCAIOLA

PASTA WITH MUSHROOM AND PINE NUT SAUCE

Ingredients

pasta (penne, fusilli, spaghetti) 400 g
ripe (plum) tomatoes 200-300 g
pancetta (dried bacon) 50-80 g
porcini mushrooms 400-500 g
dry white wine 100-200 ml
pine nuts 1-2 tbsp
olive oil 3-4 tbsp
salt, pepper
parsley

Preparation

Clean the mushrooms and chop them finely, or slice them thinly, or cut them into chunks.

Dice the pancetta (bacon). Chop the pine nuts, garlic and parsley. Peel the tomatoes and cut them into small pieces.

In a saucepan fry the mushrooms in oil. After a while add the garlic. Mix a couple of times and then pour in the wine. Let it evaporate, cooking over medium heat for 3-4 minutes. Then add the tomatoes.

Cover the pan and bring the tomatoes to a low simmer. Cook for another 10-20 minutes.

In the meantime, fry briefly the pancetta and the pine nuts in oil, over medium heat. Add them to the mushrooms, putting in also the parsley, salt and pepper. Continue cooking just for a few moments, over low heat.

Cook the pasta in an abundant quantity of salted water.

Drain the pasta "al dente" (firm to the bite), mix it with the sauce and serve it immediately.

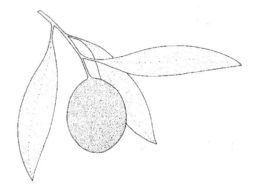

Optional ingredients: ham instead of pancetta.

Optional herbs and spices: onion instead of garlic, black olives, cream, peperoncino chili peppers, sausages.

Possible omissions: pine nuts, wine.

PASTA ALLE FAVE

PASTA WITH BROAD BEANS

Ingredients

pasta (penne, fusilli, spaghetti) 400 g

broad beans 500 g
olive oil 4-5 tbsp
garlic 1-2 cloves
salt, pepper
parsley

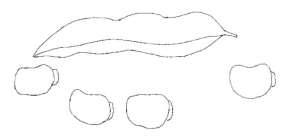

Preparation

Chop the garlic and parsley. Fry them briefly in a saucepan, over low heat.

Add the broad beans, fresh or frozen, entire or cut into pieces.

Continue cooking for 20-30 minutes over medium heat. Stir from time to time, pouring some water if necessary.

Cook the pasta in an abundant quantity of salted water.

Drain the pasta "al dente" (firm to the bite), mix it with the sauce and serve it immediately.

Optional primary ingredients: pancetta (dried bacon), prosciutto ham, tomatoes, green onions, green beans, peas, potatoes, scampi or shrimp tails.

Optional herbs and spices: fried onions, vegetable powder bouillon, chili peppers, mint, onions, cream, thyme, rosemary, grated cheese, bay leaves, pine nuts, desalted anchovy fillets, basil, marjoram, carrots, tomato paste, dry white wine, oregano, paprika powder, mustard.

PASTA AL RAGÙ DI CARNE

PASTA WITH MEAT RAGÙ

Ingredients

pasta (penne, fusilli, spaghetti) 400 g
minced (beef or pork) meat 800 g
ripe (plum) tomatoes 500 g
tomato paste 2-3 oz
olive oil 4-5 tbsp
garlic 2-3 cloves
bay leaves 3-7
salt, pepper
onions 1-2
parsley

Preparation

In a pan warm up the oil. Put in the finely chopped onions and let them fry over low heat. Then add the garlic, previously crushed or minced, as well as the finely chopped parsley. Stir a couple of times, still over low heat. Then add the meat and increase the heat to medium high.

Cook for 10-15 minutes, stirring often. Add the tomatoes, already cut into small pieces, the tomato paste and the bay leaves.

Cook for half an hour, over medium heat. Stir every now and then. If necessary, pour in some water, not much. At the end, season with salt and pepper.

Cook the pasta in an abundant quantity of salted water. Drain the pasta "al dente" (firm to the bite), mix it with the ragù and serve it at once.

Optional ingredients: sausages, mushrooms fresh or dry, chicken livers.

Optional herbs and spices: carrot, celery, red or dry white wine, sugar, pancetta (dried bacon), prosciutto ham, shallots, meat soup, nutmeg, cloves, cinnamon, grated lemon zest, milk, basil, green olives, sage, rosemary, vegetable soup powder.

Optional ingredients at the end: grated cheese, cream.

Possible omissions: garlic, parsley.

PASTA AL FORMAGGIO

PASTA WITH CHEESE SAUCE

Ingredients

pasta (penne, fusilli, spaghetti) 400 g
grated cheese
(pecorino, parmigiano o grana)
150-200 g
butter or olive oil 5-7 tbsp
milk 2-2.5 cups
nutmeg
flour
salt

Preparation

Melt the butter in a saucepan, over low heat. Take the pan off the stove and then stir in the flour. Put the pan back to the stove and cook for 1-2 minutes more, mixing constantly.

Move the pan again away from the heat and pour in the milk. Mix for a minute and put the pan back to the stove. Cover it and continue cooking for about ten minutes, still over low heat, letting the sauce to thicken gradually. Stir every now and then.

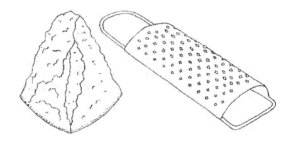

Once again remove the pan from the flame and add the grated cheese, grated nutmeg and later on even some salt (only if really necessary).

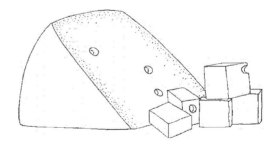

Blend the ingredients well, making sure that the sauce does not become too dense.

If needed, thin the sauce with water.

Cook the pasta in an abundant quantity of salted water.

Drain the pasta "al dente" (firm to the bite), mix it with the sauce and serve it immediately.

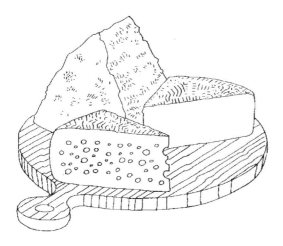

2ⁿᵈ style

In a bowl blend grated cheese, cream, olive oil, egg yolk(s), (warm) bechamel sauce, salt and pepper.

3ʳᵈ style

In a saucepan warm up oil or butter, over low heat. Add cream or milk, and later on some grated cheese.

Dissolve the cheese in the sauce and add grated nutmeg (or lemon juice, chives or parsley).

The bain marie method ("double-boiler" method, "a bagnomaria")

Dice the cheese (fontina, gorgonzola or provolone). Melt some butter in a pot (over another larger pot with hot water). Add some milk or cream and the diced cheese. Mix for a minute or two and then add a couple of egg yolks, rapidly mixing. Continue heating of the lower pot, letting the sauce to thicken. If necessary, add more milk. At the and, season with freshly ground pepper.

Note: The bain marie method of warming the food denotes the use of a water bath either for keeping cooked food warm or for cooking without allowing the ingredients to be in direct contact with the heat of the stove. It usually implies the use of two pots, one with the water, the other with the food.

Mixing, without warming up

The cheese sauce can be prepared mixing fresh cheese, oil or melted butter, vegetables or aromatic herbs (finely chopped) and herbs and spices (parsley, capers, onions, green olives, bell peppers, mustard, brandy, ...).

Type of cheese to select: grana padano, parmigiano reggiano, pecorino romano, gorgonzola, brie, robiola, fontina, provolone, asiago, mozzarella, taleggio, ...

Optional ingredients: fresh cheese, ricotta cheese, olive oil, sage, minced prosciutto ham or pancetta, lemon juice, parsley, rocket salad, paprika, sweet wine, tomato purèe or passata, mint, chives, capers, salted anchovies, fried grated onions, pistachio, basil, worcester sauce, mustard, tabasco sauce, oregano, thyme, scallions or young onions, chopped and fried, walnuts, chopped finely, cream.

PASTA AL FORMAGGIO GRATTUGIATO
PASTA WITH GRATED CHEESE SAUCE

Ingredients

pasta (penne, fusilli, spaghetti) 400 g
grated cheese
(pecorino, parmigiano o grana)
100-200 g
olive oil 5-6 tbsp

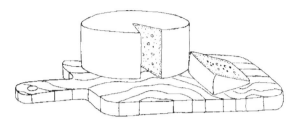

Preparation

In a bowl mix the oil and the grated cheese. Leave it to macerate for half an hour.

Cook the pasta in an abundant quantity of salted water. Drain the pasta "al dente" (firm to the bite), mix it with the cheese sauce.

Optional ingredients: basil, parsley, paprika powder, salt, pepper.

PASTA
AL
BURRO E FORMAGGIO

PASTA WITH BUTTER AND CHEESE

Ingredients

pasta (penne, fusilli, spaghetti) 400 g
grated cheese 100-200 g
butter 200 g
pepper

Preparation

Keep the butter in fresh water for a couple of hours, at room temperature.

Cook the pasta in an abundant quantity of salted water. Drain the pasta "al dente" (firm to the bite) and transfer it into a warm bowl. Mix in the butter, cut into pieces just moments before. Then blend in the grated cheese and pepper.

Optional herbs and spices: cream, peas, nutmeg, ham, prosciutto ham, pancetta (dried bacon), garlic, parsley.

Optional proceeding: If needed, pour some cooking liquid, before adding the cheese.

PASTA
CON
GAMBERI
E ZUCCHINE

PASTA WITH SHRIMPS
AND ZUCCHINI

Ingredients

pasta (penne, fusilli, spaghetti) 400 g
cooking cream 100-200 ml
shrimp tails 300-500 g
olive oil 3-4 tbsp
garlic 1-2 cloves
zucchini 2-4
salt, pepper

Preparation

Wash and cut the zucchini into (rather small) cubes. Cook them for 1-2 minu-tes in salted water and then drain them. Chop the garlic.

In a saucepan warm up some olive oil and briefly fry the garlic, over low he-at. Add the shrimp tails (fresh or fro-zen), and soon after that also the zu-cchini. Stir a couple of times and then let it all simmer for a few minutes, over medium heat. Eventually stir in the cream and season with salt and pepper.

Cook the pasta in an abundant quan-tity of salted water.

Drain the pasta "al dente", add it into the simmering sauce, toss it for a mi-nute or two over medium heat and serve it promptly.

Optional primary ingredients: scampi tails instead of shrimp tails.

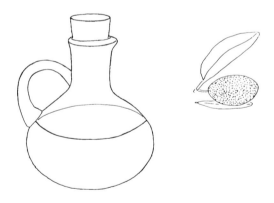

Optional herbs and spices: mint, cog-nac (brandy), dry white wine, vegeta-ble bouillon powder, tomato paste, parsley, chili peppers, saffron, onions, shallots.

Optional ingredients at the end: gra-ted cheese.

Possible omissions: garlic or cream.

PASTA AI FRUTTI DI MARE
(pasta alla pescatora, pasta di mare)
SEAFOOD PASTA

Ingredients

pasta (penne, fusilli, spaghetti) 400 g
unshelled scampi or shrimp tails 500 g
dry white wine 100-200 ml
clams and/or mussels 1 kg
tomato paste 1-2 tsp
bread crumbs 1 tbsp
olive oil 4-5 tbsp
garlic 1-3 cloves
salt, pepper
parsley

Preparation

Heat up the clams and/or mussels in pot, adding no water. When the shells open, extract the meat, saving the salt water, i.e. the seawater released by the clams (mussels).

In a saucepan warm up some oil. Put in the chopped garlic and parsley. Let them fry over low heat for a while, but not long. Then add the bread cru-mbs and continue frying for a minute or two, still over low heat.

Pour the wine and let it partly evaporate. After that add the prepared seafood and the preserved liquid. Continue cooking for 15-20 minutes, stirring periodically. Add some water if necessary. Season with salt and pepper.

Cook the pasta in an abundant quantity of salted water.

Drain the pasta "al dente", add it into the seafood sauce, toss it for a minute or two over medium heat and serve it promptly.

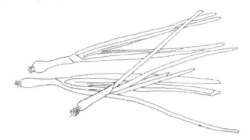

Optional herbs and spices: fried onions, desalted anchovy fillets, capers, bay leaves, paprika powder, sage, basil, lemon zest and/or juice, celery, cognac (brandy), chili peppers, chives.

Possible omissions: tomatoes, either shellfish or crab tails, wine.

SPAGHETTI ALLA TRABACCOLARA

Ingredients

spaghetti 400 g
assorted fish fillets 500-700 g
peperoncino (chili pepper) 0,5-1
dry white wine 80-150 ml
olive oil 4-5 tbsp
tomatoes 1-4
onion 1
parsley
garlic
salt

Preparation

In a saucepan warm up some oil. Put in the chopped onion, and soon after that the minced garlic and parsley. Let them fry over low heat for a while, but not long. Then add the tomatoes, already cut to pieces.

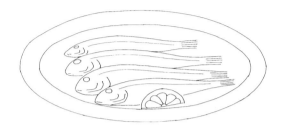

Continue cooking until the liquid evaporates and then pour in the wine. When the wine is also almost vaporised put in and the fish fillets. Season with salt and the minced peperoncino. After another 10 minutes of cooking over moderate heat, remove the pan.

Cook the pasta in an abundant quantity of salted water. Drain the pasta "al dente", and then season it with the fish sauce.

Serve the pasta with additional seasoning of minced parsley.

Other types of pasta that can be used: maltagliati, penne, fusilli.

Optional ingredients: molluscs, crab or shell meat.

Possible omissions: tomatoes.

Note: Typical dish of the Viareggio region.

PASTA ALLA BARROCCIAIA

Ingredients

spaghetti or short pasta 400 g
fresh anchovies 350-500 g
concentrated tomato paste 1-2 tbsp
peperoncino (chili pepper) 1
salted anchovy fillets 3-5
olive oil 4-5 tbsp
garlic 1-2 cloves
noci 5-10
parsley
salt

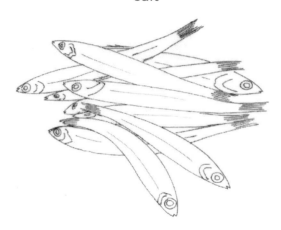

Preparation

Clean and rinse the anchovies, separating the fillets.

Pour the oil in a large pan and add the finely chopped garlic, parsley and chili pepper. Brown and then add the salted anchovy fillets.

Soon add the chopped walnuts or even better the walnuts crushed in the mortar. Stir a few times and then add the tomato paste.

Season with salt and put in the fresh anchovy fillets. Keep stirring from ti-me to time, for a minute or two, over medium heat, and then remove the sauce.

Cook the pasta in an abundant quantity of salted water.

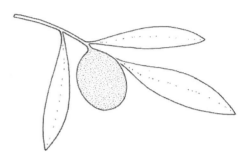

Drain the pasta "al dente", add it into the simmering sauce, toss it for a minute or two over medium heat and serve it promptly.

Optional ingredients: cherry tomatoes, pine nuts, basil, sage, pepper.

Spaghetti alla Barrocciaia, meat version: Season the pasta with a sauce prepared with meat, onions, celery, carrots, red wine, oil, pancetta (bacon), peperoncino o pepe, salt and mushrooms.

Note: The expression "alla barrocciaia" derives from the name "barrocciaio", that is the one who led the gig, a two-wheeled vehicle.

PASTA ALLA TORTELLONA

Ingredients

reginette or short pasta 400 g
chicken livers and heats 100-150 g
ground pork meat 150-200 g
ground viel meat 300-400 g
tomato passata 150-300 g
fresh sausage 100-150 g
chard 150-300 g
salt, pepper
onions 1-2
carrot 1
nutmeg
celery
egg 1

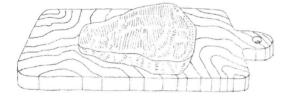

Preparation

In a saucepan warm up some oil. Put in the chopped onion. Let gently fry over low heat for quite a while. Then add the meat and the minced sausage. Put in also the grated carrot and the chopped celery, not much.

Stir for a minute or two and then pour in the wine. Let it almost evaporate. Add the tomato passata and continue cooking for a half an hour.

After that put in the chicken livers and hearts. Stir a few times and keep on cooking over moderate heat.

In the meanwhile, boil the young chard. Drain it well after boiling and after that cut it finely.

Add the chard to the sauce, add some grated nutmeg and an egg, and cook the sauce for a few minutes more.

Season the boiled pasta with the sauce and some grated cheese.

Note: Tortellona is a pasta sauce typical of Borgo a Buggiano.

PASTA AGLI AGLIETTI FRESCHI

Ingredients

spaghetti or short pasta 400 g
spring garlic plants 100-200 g
peperoncino (chili pepper) 1
fresh tomatoes 400-500 g
grated cheese 50-100 g
olive oil
basil
salt

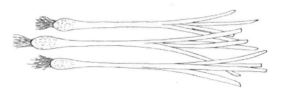

Preparation

Chop the garlic plants, including the tender part of the stems.

Fry the garlic lightly in the oil with the chilli pepper. Add the peeled and chopped tomatoes and some salt.

Cover the saucepan and continue cooking for about 10-15 minutes.

Cook the pasta in an abundant quantity of salted water.

Drain the pasta "al dente", add it into the simmering sauce, add toss it for a minute or two over medium heat. Remove the pan from the heat, stir in chopped basil and some grated cheese and serve promptly the pasta.

In the sauce obtained, drain the pasta al dente, adding chopped basil and parmesan.

Optional herbs and spices: pepper instead of peperoncino (chili pepper).

Note: In your own garden or at the green market pick the youngest garlic plants.

PASTA ALLE ACCIUGHE SOTTO SALE

PASTA WITH DESALTED ANCHOVIES

Ingredients

pasta (penne, fusilli, spaghetti) 400 g
desalted anchovy fillets 20-40
olive oil 2-3 tbsp

Preparation

In a saucepan warm up the oil. Add the anchovy fillets and let them dissolve over very low heat. As soon as it happens, immediately remove the pan from the heat.

Cook the pasta in an abundant quantity of salted water. Drain it "al dente" and season it with anchovy sauce.

Optional herbs and spices: parsley, soft inside of a bread slice, cut into small cubes, and later fried in some oil, fried onions, wild fennel leaves, bread crumbs, tomato paste, pine nuts, raisins, garlic, basil, capers, green or black olives, thyme, celery, oregano, chili peppers, vegetable bouillon powder, rosemary, bay leaves, lemon zest and juice, paprika powder.

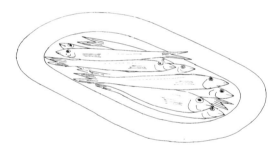

Optional: Add some some liquid preserved after the cooking the pasta.

PASTA AL TONNO SOTT'OLIO

PASTA WITH TUNA FISH

Ingredients

pasta (penne, fusilli, spaghetti) 400 g

62

canned tuna fish 250 g
olive oil 3-5 tbsp
cream 4-6 oz
salt, pepper

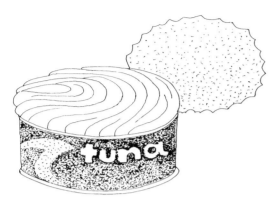

Preparation

Roughly mash the (already drained) tuna fish and add the cream, olive oil, salt and pepper.

Cook the pasta in an abundant quantity of salted water. Drain the pasta "al dente" (firm to the bite) and season with the tuna sauce.

Optional primary ingredients: canned or fried mushrooms, chopped and drained tomatoes, mozzarella cheese, (canned) artichokes, cooked vegetables (peas, corn, green peppers, cauliflower, broccoli), scampi or shrimp tails (cooked),

Optional herbs and spices: capers, garlic, parsley, dried tomatoes, tomato paste, sugar, dry white wine, oregano, mint, basil, thyme, onions, chili peppers, wild fennel, lemon zest and juice, vegetable bouillon powder, rosemary, bay leaves, black or green olives, grated cheese, desalted anchovy fillets, pine nuts, "pesto alla genovese" sauce, carrots, almonds, mayonnaise, pickled gherkins.

Possible omissions: cream.

PASTA RIPIENA
STUFFED PASTA

Ingredients

stuffed pasta (tortellini, ravioli, cappelletti o al.)
400 g
grated cheese 50-80 g
butter or olive oil 2-3 tbsp
cream 200 ml
salt

Preparation

Cook the pasta in an abundant quantity of salted water. Drain the pasta "al dente" (firm to the bite), season it with cream, butter or oil, grated cheese and salt.

Note: The stuffed pasta, cooked and drained, may be seasoned with various sauces but those sauces which are light, of delicate flavour, are considered to be the most suitable.

MACCHERONI DI CIACCIO

A unique type of pasta, rhombus-shaped, made with chestnut flour. The dough of this pasta makes it very suitable for the full-bodied sauces and the meat or game ragù.

PASTA AL FORNO
BAKED PASTA

Ingredients

pasta (penne, fusilli, spaghetti) 400 g
selected sauce and/or
aromatic herbs and spices
salt, pepper

Preparation

Cook the pasta in an abundant quantity of salted water. Drain the pasta very much "al dente" (a bit more undercooked than usual).

Grease the baking pan and line a layer of drained pasta on the bottom of the pan. Spread over it a layer of the selected sauce and the other ingredients.

Continue lining the layers of pasta and the layers of condiments. Top with bechamel sauce, tomato sauce, grated cheese or/and bread crumbs. Drizzle very lightly with olive oil.

Bake for 10-20 minutes in a preheated oven, at a rather high temperature.

Allow the pasta to rest for a few minutes before serving it.

Sauce selection: ground meat sauce, ricotta cheese, cheese sauce, seafood sauce, mushroom sauce, vegetable sauce.

Optional primary ingredients: mortadella, tomatoes, cooked potatoes, prosciutto ham, mushrooms, cooked vegetables (peas, artichokes, eggplants, broad beans), cooked eggs, beaten eggs, cheese (mozzarella, ricotta or other), desalted anchovy fillets, pancetta (dried bacon), bell peppers, ground meat, canned tuna fish.

Optional herbs and spices: onions, green onions, basil, chives, bechamel sauce, grated cheese, green or black olives, cream, parsley, chili peppers, nutmeg, garlic, oregano, celery, thyme, rosemary, marjoram, bay leaves, sage, dry white wine.

LASAGNE
LASAGNA

Ingredients

dry lasagne pasta sheets 500 g
bechamel sauce
grated cheese
meat ragù

Preparation

Cook the pasta sheets in an abundant quantity of salted water. Drain the pasta still very much "al dente" (a bit undercooked).

Grease the baking pan and line a layer of drained pasta on the bottom of the pan. Spread over it layers of ragù, bechamel sauce and grated cheese.

Continue lining the layers of pasta and other ingredients. Top with bechamel sauce, tomato sauce and grated cheese. Drizzle very lightly with olive oil.

Bake for 20-40 minutes in a preheated oven, at a rather high temperature.

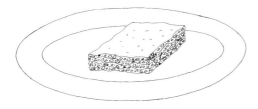

Allow the baked pasta ("lasagne alla bolognese") to rest for 5-10 minutes before serving it.

Optional ingredients: mushrooms sauce, cheese sauce, cooked vegetables (artichokes, zucchini, green beans, peas, tomatoes, potatoes, eggplants or other), prosciutto ham, cheese (mozzarella, ricotta, mascarpone or other).

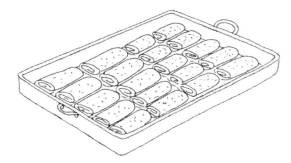

Cannelloni

Cook the pasta sheets (drain it some-

what undercooked), and then spread over every sheet a relatively thin layer of the chosen filling (ragù, bechamel sauce, grated cheese, mushroom sauce, seafood sauce or other).

Roll up the filled pasta shaping the cannelloni and then bake them.

Note: "Le lasagne bastarde alla Lunigiana" is a particular type of pasta because the dough is prepared with wheat and chestnut flour.

PASTA ALLE POLPETTINE

PASTA WITH MEATBALLS

Ingredients

pasta
penne, fusilli or tagliatelle 400 g
ground beef or veal 200-300 g
vegetable bouillon powder
tomato passata 250-500 g
ground pork 200-300 g
olive oil 5-7 tbsp
garlic cloves 2-4
bread crumbs
milk 3-4 tbsp
salt, pepper
sugar 1 tsp
nutmeg
onion 1
parsley
eggs 2

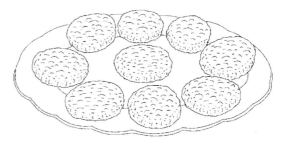

Preparation

In a large bowl mix the ground meat, beaten eggs, ground nutmeg, vegetable bouillon powder, minced parsley, minced garlic, bread crumbs, milk, salt and pepper. Shape the meat balls, not big, and roll them in the bread crumbs.

In a pot heat some olive oil and let the chopped onions fry for a couple of minutes over moderate heat, stirring occasionally.

In a pan heat the oil and fry every meatball, both sides, over medium heat, but not long.

Arrange the superficially fried meatballs in the pot with onions and pour in the tomato passata and sugar (but not much). Cook for 30-45 minutes, over medium heat, until the meatballs are cooked. Shake the pot occasionally. Do not stir. Use the meatballs and the sauce to season the boiled and drained pasta.

BRINGOLI

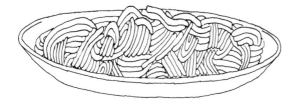

Thick and long spaghettoni made with water and flour (sometimes with the addition of corn).

Also called brigonzoli or bringuilli, the bringoli are typical of the Arezzo area.

CIRIOLE

In the Val di Chiana and in the province of Siena, we find ciriole, spaghettoni with an irregular shape, usually served with meat sauce, vegetable sauces like tomato sauce, a cream with porcini mushrooms or with four cheeses, butter and sage.

TORDELLI

In the whole province of Lucca the meat ravioli are called tordelli, and not tortelli as in most of the rest of Italy.

TORTELLI MAREMMANI

Tortelli are larger ravioli. Stuffed with ricotta and spinach, they are handmade and seasoned strictly with meat sauce.

PANNICELLI ARETINI

The pannicelli arettini are large ravioli filled with ricotta, spinach or chard, grated cheese, salt and pepper. They are not boiled, as pasta usually is, but cooked in the oven with a tomato sauce or with butter, parmesan and cinnamon.

MALFATTI

Malfatti is a traditional first course, the irregular gnocchi made with ricotta and spinach served with melted butter and grated cheese. The generous dimensions of these dumplings would suggest serving four of them per serving.

RICE

Following the wheat, the rice is the second most important nutrition source in the world.

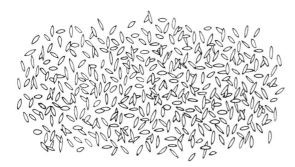

Italy is the leading rice producer in the European Union.

Although Italy accounts for less than 1 percent of the global rice production, it is the fourth-largest rice-exporting country after Thailand, United States and India.

For the purpose of cooking a risotto, use only the best quality rice.

Risotto rice is divided into four categories based on the length of the grain: commune, semifino, fino and superfino.

The most commonly used for risotto would be the rice in the so called "riso superfino" category: riso Carnaroli, Vialone Nano, Baldo, Roma, Arborio.

RISI
E
BISI

RICE AND PEAS

Ingredients

rice 200-300 g
pancetta (dried bacon) 50-80 g
vegetable broth 1 l
or
vegetable bouillon powder 1 tbsp
grated cheese 3-5 tbsp
olive oil 3-4 tbsp
peas 1 kg / 2 lb
butter 30-50 g
salt, pepper
onion 1
parsley

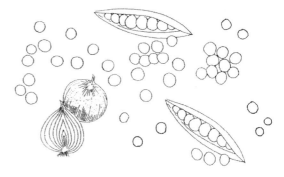

Preparation

Chop finely the onion and the parsley.

In a pot warm up the oil. Gently fry the onions, adding soon also the parsley, over low heat.

Stir a few times and put in the peas. Cover the pot and increase the heat to medium high.

After 2-3 minutes, stir in the rice (already separately fried with some oil for a minute or two).

Continue cooking over medium heat, adding some warm broth or water every now and then. Stir often. Season with salt and pepper.

Cook the rice until it is tender, but still firm to the bite. Off heat, stir in the butter and the grated cheese. Serve after a couple of minutes of rest.

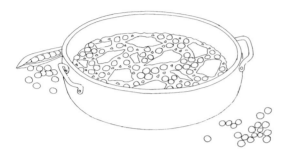

Optional primary ingredients: ground meat, mushrooms, broad beans, leeks, tomatoes, artichokes, green beans, cuttlefish, canned tuna, scampi or shrimp tails, zucchini, green onions.

Optional herbs and spices: garlic, tomato paste, ham, bread crumbs, wild fennel leaves, chives, green onions, mint, nutmeg, carrots, cream, vegetable bouillon powder, cloves, marjoram, chili peppers, basil, celery, lemon zest and juice, capers, dry white wine.

Optional ingredients at the end: parsley, mint, grated cheese, ricotta, eggs beaten with lemon zest and juice.

Possible omissions: garlic, pancetta (dried bacon) or onions.

Suggestions: The dish should not be as dry as a normal risotto. It should have the density of a rather dense vegetable soup.

Optional proceeding: Pea pods (green), cooked and mashed into puré, may also be included, before adding the rice.

Different method: Cook the peas and the rice separately and then mix them.

RISOTTO ALLE VERDURE
(risotto alla paesana)
RISOTTO WITH VEGETABLES

Ingredients

rice 250-350 g
pancetta (dried bacon) 60-150 g
broad beans 100-200 g
olive oil 4-5 tbsp
peas100-200 g
ripe tomato 1
salt, pepper
celery rib 1
zucchini 1
carrot 1
onion 1
parsley
butter

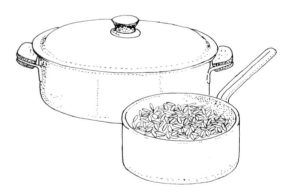

Preparation

In a saucepan warm up the oil. Fry chopped onions over low heat. Then add the diced pancetta, stir a couple of times and proceed with adding (one by one) all the vegetables, already cut to pieces. Cook for 5-6 minutes over medium heat.

Stir in the rice (already separately fried with some oil for a minute or two).

Continue cooking over medium heat, adding some warm broth or water every now and then. Stir often. Season with salt and pepper.

Cook the rice until it is tender, but still firm to the bite. Off heat, stir in the butter and the chopped parsley. Serve after a couple of minutes of rest.

Optional ingredients: artichokes, eggplants, potatoes, leeks, green beans, bell peppers, mushrooms, red lentils, tomatoes, corn, green onions, scampi or shrimp tails, cauliflower, cooked beans.

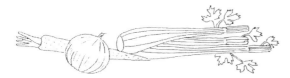

Optional herbs and spices: garlic, vegetable bouillon powder, sage, basil, wild fennel, chili peppers, bay leaves, red or dry white wine, lemon zest or juice, saffron, black or green olives, capers, marjoram, thyme, nutmeg, paprika powder, rosemary, sweet wine.

Optional ingredients at the end: grated cheese, rocket salad, green onions, garlic, parsley, cream.

Possible omissions: pancetta or celery.

Riso e verdure
(rice and vegetables)

Cook separately the rice and each of the chosen vegetables. Mix all the cooked and afterwards drained ingredients. Season with salt, pepper, butter and other condiments.

Note: When rice and other ingredient(s) are being cooked separately and then later on mixed together, and that is done often, the strict "cucina italiana" does not consider such a dish to be a *risotto*. It is considered to be a *"rice and ..."* dish, as in above mentioned case it is the "riso e verdure". For example, there is also a difference between the "risotto with mushrooms" (in which case the rice is cooked in the mushroom sauce and water) and the "rice and mushrooms" (in which case the rice and the mushroom sauce are being cooked separately). However, there are exceptions ("risi e bisi", for instance, which is not called a "risotto", but it is usually cooked as a classic, although low-density, risotto).

RISOTTO AL POMODORO

RISOTTO WITH TOMATOES

Ingredients

rice 250-350 g
ripe tomatoes 500 g – 1 kg
olive oil 3-4 tbsp
salt, pepper
sugar ½ tsp
onions 1-2
butter

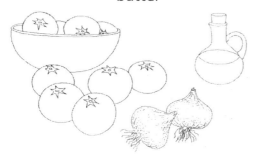

Preparation

Peel the tomatoes and cut them into small pieces. Chop finely the onions.

In a saucepan warm up the oil and fry the onions, over low heat. Then add the tomatoes. Increase the heat to medium and let the tomatoes cook for 5-10 minutes. Then stir in the rice (already separately fried with some oil for a minute).

Continue cooking over medium heat, adding some warm broth or water every now and then. Stir often. Season with salt and pepper.

Cook the rice until it is tender, but still firm to the bite. Off heat, stir in the butter. Serve after a couple of minutes of rest.

Optional herbs and spices: garlic, parsley, basil, carrot, cloves, celery, bay leaves, nutmeg, pancetta (dried bacon), dry white wine, prosciutto ham, sage, paprika powder, vegetable bouillon powder.

Optional ingredients at the end: grated cheese, basil, parsley.

RISOTTO AI FUNGHI

RISOTTO WITH MUSHROOMS

Ingredients

rice 250-350 g / 8-11 oz
cream 50-80 ml / 2-3 oz
mushrooms 500 g / 1 lb
olive oil 4-5 tbsp
salt, pepper
butter

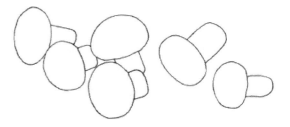

Preparation

Clean, briefly rinse and then thinly slice the mushrooms. Braise the mushrooms with some oil, over moderate heat, stirring often.

Let most of the liquid evaporate. Right after that, stir in the rice (already separately fried for a minute or two, with some oil).

Continue cooking over medium heat, adding some warm broth or water every now and then. Stir often.

Cook the rice until it is tender, but still firm to the bite. Minute or two before the end, add the cream. Off heat, stir in the butter. Season with salt and pepper. Serve after a couple of minutes of rest.

ons, eggs, egg yolks, cooked eggs, celery, pancetta (dried bacon), chives, tomatoes, oregano, paprika powder, saffron, marjoram, bay leaves, (fresh) cheese, ricotta cheese, capers, sage, basil, thyme, mint, sugar, rosemary, rocket salad, nutmeg, black or green olives, red or dry white wine, sweet wine, lemon zest and juice, vinegar, bechamel sauce, sour cream, mustard, truffle oil.

Optional ingredients at the end: grated cheese.

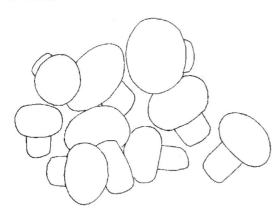

Optional primary ingredients: milk instead of cream, (ground) meat, artichokes, bell peppers, peas, chicken livers, leeks, shrimp or scampi tails, dry mushrooms.

Optional herbs and spices: vegetable bouillon powder, garlic, parsley, chili peppers, shallots, carrots, green oni-

RISOTTO AI PEPERONI

RISOTTO WITH BELL PEPPERS

Ingredients

rice 250-350 g / 8-11 oz
yellow bell pepper 1
green bell pepper 1
ripe tomatoes 1-2
olive oil 4-5 tbsp
red bell pepper 1
garlic 1-2 cloves
onions 1-2
butter
salt

Preparation

Cut the bell peppers into small cubes. Chop finely the onions and garlic. Peel the tomatoes and cut them into small pieces.

In a saucepan warm up the oil and fry the onions, over low heat. Then increase the heat and add the rice. Let it fry for a minute or two. Stir constantly. After that, add the bell peppers and tomatoes.

Continue cooking over medium heat, adding some warm broth or water every now and then, when needed. Stir often. Season with salt and pepper.

Cook the rice until it is tender, but still firm to the bite. Off heat, stir in the butter. Serve after a couple of minutes of rest.

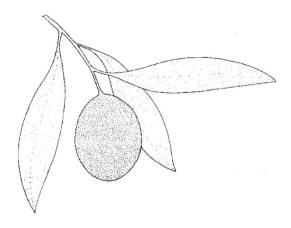

Optional primary ingredients: zucchini, black or green olives, canned tuna, sausages.

Optional herbs and spices: dry white wine, cream, pancetta (dried bacon), parsley, vegetable bouillon powder, basil, capers, oregano, rosemary, thyme, bay leaves.

Optional ingredients at the end: grated cheese.

Possible omissions: tomatoes, onions or garlic.

Different method: Mix the separately cooked rice and the gently fried bell peppers (with o without garlic, onions and/or tomatoes). Add butter or oil, season with salt and pepper.

RISOTTO AL FORMAGGIO
(risotto bianco)
RISOTTO WITH CHEESE

Ingredients

rice 250-350 g
grated cheese
(parmigiano, grana, pecorino, gorgonzola or other)
70-150 g
dry white wine 100-120 ml
olive oil 3-4 tbsp
salt, pepper
butter

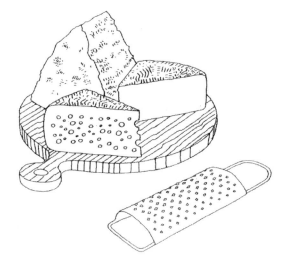

Preparation

Warm up the oil and put in the rice. Let it fry for a minute, stirring it constantly. After that, pour in the wine and let it almost evaporate.

eat and love Tuscany

Continue cooking over medium heat, adding some warm broth or water every now and then, when needed. Stir often.

Cook the rice until it is tender, but firm to the bite. Off heat, stir in the cheese and butter. Season with salt and pepper. Serve after a couple of minutes of rest.

Optional herbs and spices: onions, green onions, shallots, nutmeg, vegetable bouillon powder, basil, parsley, orange juice, cream, garlic.

Possible omissions: dry white wine.

RISOTTO
AL
RAGÙ DI CARNE
RISOTTO
WITH GROUND MEAT SAUCE

Ingredients

rice 250-350 g
minced (beef or pork) meat 800 g
ripe (plum) tomatoes 500 g
tomato paste 2-3 oz
olive oil 4-5 tbsp
garlic 2-3 cloves
bay leaves 3-7
salt, pepper
onions 1-2
parsley

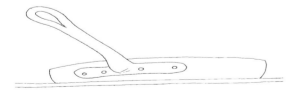

Preparation

In a saucepan fry the chopped onions, over low heat, adding soon also the chopped garlic and parsley.

Put in the meat and stir for a few minutes. After that add the tomatoes. Season with salt, pepper and bay leaves.

Let the meat cook for approximately one hour. Then stir in the rice (already separately fried for a minute or two, with some oil).

Continue cooking over medium heat, adding some warm broth or water every now and then. Stir often.

Cook the rice until it is tender, but still firm to the bite. Season with salt and pepper. Serve after a couple of minutes of rest.

Optional herbs and spices: sausages, dry mushrooms, pancetta (dried bacon), ham, red or dry white wine, celery, carrot, cloves, vegetable bouillon powder, sugar, nutmeg, lemon zest, basil, rosemary, cinnamon, milk.

Optional ingredients at the end: grated cheese, cream.

Possible omissions: garlic or parsley.

Different method: Mix the (already completely prepared) ragù with the rice only when it is almost cooked.

RISOTTO NERO
(risotto con le seppie)
RISOTTO WITH CUTTLEFISH

Ingredients

rice 250-350 g / 8-11 oz
cuttlefish 1 kg / 2 lb
ripe tomatoes 1-2
olive oil 4-5 tbsp
garlic 2-3 cloves
salt, pepper
onions1-2
parsley
butter

Preparation

Clean the cuttlefish and cut it into pieces, but not too small. Save the ink bags by putting them into a cup and diluting the ink with some water, fish broth, dry white wine or oil.

Chop the onions, garlic and parsley.

In a saucepan fry the onions over low heat. Before long, add the garlic and parsley. Stir a couple of times and put in the cuttlefish and tomatoes. Cook for a few minutes over medium heat and then stir in the rice (already separately fried for a minute or two, with some oil).

Continue cooking over medium heat, adding some warm broth or water every now and then. Stir often. A couple of minutes before the end, add the diluted cuttlefish ink.

Cook the rice until it is tender, but firm to the bite. Off heat, stir in the butter. Serve after a couple of minutes of rest.

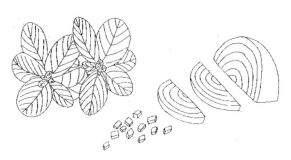

Optional primary ingredients: (yellow) bell peppers, tomato paste instead of fresh tomatoes, squid (calamari), clam or mussel meat, scampi or shrimp tail meat, mushrooms, almonds, broad beans, peas.

Optional herbs and spices: red or dry white wine, sweet wine, vinegar, cognac (brandy), chili peppers, balsamic vinegar (aceto balsamico), cream, lemon zest and juice, celery, thyme, basil, capers, sugar, rosemary, green or black olives, cheese, honey, vegetable bouillon powder, desalted anchovy fillets.

Optional ingredients at the end: grated cheese.

Possible omissions: cuttlefish ink, tomatoes.

RISOTTO CON GLI SCAMPI

RISOTTO WITH SCAMPI

Ingredients

rice 250-350 g
unshelled scampi (tails) 1-1,5 kg
cognac (armagnac, brandy) 1-2 tbsp
dry white wine 100 ml
bread crumbs 2 tbsp
tomato paste 1 tsp
olive oil 4-5 tbsp
garlic 2-3 cloves
salt, pepper
parsley

Preparation

In a pan warm up the oil. Gently fry the finely chopped garlic and parsley.

Later on add the crumbs. Fry still over low heat, not more than minute. Then add the scampi (tails). Stir a couple of times and pour in the wine. Add the tomato paste, as well as the salt and pepper. Pour also some water, taking care not to surpass the upper level of the ingredients in the pan. Add a tablespoon of cognac.

Continue cooking over medium heat, for 5-10 minutes. Then stir in the rice (already separately fried for a minute or two, with some oil). Keep cooking, stirring very often. Every now and then, add some warm fish broth (or the broth prepared with the discarded scampi body parts, intestines excluded), or warm water.

Cook the rice until it is tender, but still firm to the bite. Off heat, stir in the butter. Serve after a couple of minutes of rest.

Optional primary ingredients: cuttlefish, clam or mussel meat, (yellow) bell peppers, mushrooms, zucchini, peas, desalted anchovy fillets.

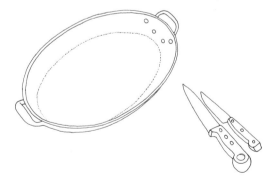

Optional herbs and spices: shallots, thyme, marjoram, paprika powder, vegetable bouillon powder, cloves, chili peppers, rosemary, almonds, bay leaves, sugar, lemon zest and/or juice, pine nuts, saffron, onions, green onions, sage, carrots, mustard, sweet wine, chives, celery.

Optional ingredients at the end: grated cheese, cream, rocket salad.

Note: The same recipe is also used for the preparation of the famous "seafood risotto" ("risotto ai frutti di mare") in which case the scampi should be accompanied by some clams or/and mussels, possibly shrimp tail meat and perhaps even squid or cuttlefish meat.

RISOTTO AI GAMBERI

RISOTTO WITH SHRIMPS

Ingredients

shelled shrimp tail meat
(fresh or frozen) 400-750 g
olive oil 4-5 cucchiai
salt, pepper
lemons 1-3
onion 1
butter

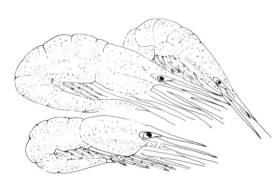

Preparation

In a pan fry the chopped onion, over low heat. Add the shelled shrimp tails and lemon zest. Stir a few times and pour in the rice (already separately fried with some oil for a minute or two).

Continue cooking over medium heat, adding some warm broth or water every now and then. Stir often. Season with salt and pepper.

Cook the rice until it is tender, but still firm to the bite. Off heat, stir in the butter. Serve after a couple of minutes of rest.

Optional ingredients: zucchini.

Optional herbs and spices: vegetable bouillon powder, garlic, parsley, bread crumbs, dry white wine, cognac (brandy), shallots, carrots,

Optional ingredients at the end: grated cheese, lemon juice, cream.

Possible omissions: lemon zest.

RISOTTO CON LE CONCHIGLIE

RISOTTO

WITH CLAMS OR MUSSELS

Ingredients

fresh unshelled clams or/and mussels
1,5-2 kg
olive oil 4-5 cucchiai
garlic 1-2 cloves
bread crumbs
salt, pepper
parsley
butter

Preparation

In a large pan heat up the clams or/and mussels. Then extract the meat from the shells. Filtrate the liquid that has remained after that.

In a pan warm up some oil and gently fry the finely chopped parsley and garlic, over low heat. Soon add the bread crumbs and stir a few times. Then put the clam (mussel) meat, stir for a minute, and pour in the rice (already separately fried with some oil for a minute or two). Continue cooking over medium heat, adding some warm preserved liquid every now and then. Stir often. Season with salt and pepper.

Cook the rice until it is tender, but still firm to the bite. Off heat, stir in the butter. Serve after a couple of minutes of rest.

Optional primary ingredients: zucchini, (yellow) bell peppers, broad beans.

Optional herbs and spices: tomato paste, dry white wine, chili peppers, fried onions, desalted anchovy fillets, black or green olives, cloves, marjoram, lemon zest and/or juice, basil, capers, oregano, chives, saffron.

Optional ingredients at the end: grated cheese, cream, rocket salad, egg yolks.

ARANCINI DI RISO

RICE BALLS

Ingredients

Filling:

tomato paste 1-3 tbsp
ground (minced) meat 150-200 g / 5-7 oz
cheese provola, scamorza, caciocavallo or mozzarella 150 g / 5 oz
red wine 100 ml / ½ cup
peas 80-100 g /3 oz
olive oil 5-6 tbsp
salt, pepper
butter 1 oz
onion 1

Rice:

rice 400-450 g / 1 lb
grated cheese 50 g / 2 oz
butter 30 g / 1 oz
egg yolks 3
saffron

Coating:

bread crumbs
eggs 2

Frying:

frying oil

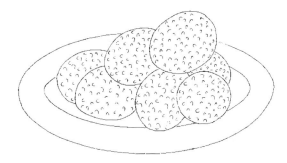

Preparation

In a pot warm up 1-25 quarts of salted water. Pour in the rice and let it cook. Drain the cooked rice and stir in the butter, saffron, egg yolks and grated cheese. Leave it to rest for a couple of hours.

In the meantime, cook the peas in a quart of water.

In a pan warm up the butter with the oil and the finely chopped onion, over low heat. Add the meat, increase the heat to medium, and fry for a minute or two, stirring constantly. Then pour in the wine and let it almost evaporate. Add the tomato paste and some water.

Continue cooking for 15-20 minutes over moderate heat. Season with salt and pepper. Remove the pan from the heat and stir in the cooked peas.

Cut the chosen cheese(s) into small cubes.

In the palm of one hand flatten a small quantity of rice and form a circle, rather thin. In the center of the circle put a small quantity of the meat and pea filling and 1-2 cheese cubes. Cover the filled rice with some more rice and form a small ball.

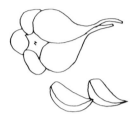

Roll the arancini balls in the beaten eggs and after that in the bread crumbs.

Fry the balls in an abbundant quantity of oil, not many at the same time. A minute or two later, remove them from the oil and lay them on paper towels to drain the oil.

Optional primary ingredients for the meat: garlic, cloves, bay leaves, dry white instead of red wine, vegetable bouillon powder.

Optional proceeding: before rolling the balls in the eggs, roll them in flour.

Note: Instead of filling the rice balls with meat, fill them with cheese, prosciutto ham or ricotta cheese with spinach.

eat and love Tuscany

FISH
&
SEAFOOD

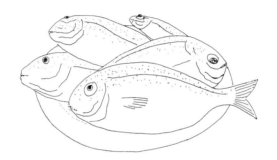

TRIGLIE ALLA LIVORNESE

Ingredients

mullets (triglie) 1 kg
tomato passata or paste 3-4 tbsp
olive oil 4-5 tbsp
bay leaves 1-2
garlic 1 clove
salt, pepper
onion 1
parsley
flour

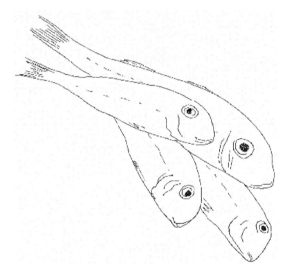

Preparation

Clean, rinse, drain and then roll in flour the red mullets.

Pour a little oil in a saucepan. Fry the fish superficially on both sides. Remove the mullets and set them aside.

In the same saucepan, in olive oil, fry the chopped parsley, garlic, onion, bay leaves, salt and pepper, over low heat. After a few minutes add the to-mato passata, stir and then put back the fish. Raise the heat a little.

Optional additions: sugar, chili, thyme, celery, fresh tomatoes instead of passata, fennel seeds.

Tips: Shake the casserole from time to time, without stirring the fish.

CACCIUCCO ALLA LIVORNESE

FISH STEW, LIVORNO STYLE

Ingredients

(assorted) fish 2 kg
squid, cuttlefish and/or small octopus 500 g
scampi, shrimps and/or small lobsters 500 g
mussels and/or clams 500 g
olio d'oliva 6-7 cucchiai
red wine 200-300 ml
ripe tomatoes 500g
garlic 3-5 cloves
vinegar 1-3 tbsp
bay leaves 1-3
chili pepper 1
celery 2 ribs
salt, pepper
onions 1-3
carrot 1
parsley

Preparation

Scale, gut and rinse the fish. Clean the shellfish, molluscs and crustaceans. Cut the big fish into pieces. Chop the onion, garlic, celery and parsley. Grate the carrot. Peel the tomatoes and cut them into small pieces.

In a large saucepan, heat the oil and fry the onion, garlic, celery and parsley. Then add the carrot, bay leaves and chilli. Put the molluscs, crustaceans and cuttlefish.

Cook for a couple of minutes and then pour in the vinegar and wine. Let it almost evaporate and add the tomatoes. Season with salt and pepper.

Cook over medium heat for 10-15 minutes. After that lay the fish down, too. Cook for 10-20 minutes over moderate heat.

Serve in soup plates with slices of toasted bread (rubbed with garlic).

The cacciucco is best enjoyed not too hot, when the bread is completely soaked in the soup.

Note: The city of Livorno celebrates it famous traditional dish in june each year by organizing a festival named "Cacciuco Pride".

CACCIUCCO ALLA VIAREGGINA

FISH STEW, VIAREGGIO STYLE

Ingredients

(assorted) fish 2 kg
squid, cuttlefish and/or small octopus 500 g
scampi, shrimps and/or small lobsters 500 g
mussels and/or clams 500 g
concentrated tomato paste 2-4 tbsp
peperoncino (chili pepper) 1olio d'oliva 6-7 cucchiai
garlic 3-5 cloves
salt

Preparation

Scale, gut and rinse the fish. Clean the shellfish, molluscs and crustaceans.

Cut the big fish into pieces. Chop the onion, garlic, celery and parsley. Grate the carrot. Peel the tomatoes and cut them into small pieces.

Using the discarded parts of the fish, crostaceans, molluscs and shellfish, heads and other, intestines excluded, boil a thick soup, to be used later during the preparation of the "cacciucco". After a half an hour of cooking, filter the soup.

Put all the ingredients to be boiled In the prepared soup, other than the fish. After 30-40 minutes of cooking over medium heat, add the tomatoe paste (or fresh tomatoes, or passata), garlic clove, olive oil, salt and peperoncino. Continue cooking over moderate heat for 5-10 minutes.

The Viareggio style cacciucco is served on a mat of toasted bread slices spread over a large serving plate.

PESCE
AL
CARTOCCIO

BAKED WRAPPED FISH

Ingredients

fish (whole or fillets) 1250 g
aluminum (or parchment or other)
roasting paper
selected herbs and spices
olive oil 4-5 tbsp
salt

Preparation

Clean and rinse the fish. Sprinkle the roasting paper with salt and spatter some olive oil. Place the fish on the roasting paper. Season the fish (inside and out) with selected herbs and spices. After that spatter some oil over the surface of the fish and then fold up the roasting paper.

Place the wrapped fish in a baking dish. Put it into a preheated oven and bake for 15-45 minutes (depending on the fish size) over medium heat.

Optional ingredients: squid, cuttlefish, scampi, shrimps, mussels or clams (shelled), grapes, black or green olives, tomatoes, potatoes, bell pepper, zucchini, eggplants, pickled gherkins, carrots, desalted anchovy fillets.

Optional herbs and spices: rosemary, oregano, sage, basil, thyme, parsley, garlic, tomato paste or "passata", lemon zest or juice, dry white wine, butter, cognac (brandy), pepper, orange slices, lemon slices, bay leaves, onions, celery, cloves, wild fennel, marjoram, bread crumbs (previously fried in some oil), tomato sauce, capers.

Optional proceeding: Seasoned fish fillets may be rolled up later, before being placed on the roasting paper.

Note: It is not obligatory to season the fish before wrapping and baking it. The fish may be seasoned after the baking (with salt, oil, parsley ...).

ACCIUGHE LESSE AL LIMONE

BOILED ANCHOVIES WITH LEMON JUICE

Ingredients

anchovies 1 kg
olive oil 5-6 tbsp
lemons 1-2
salt

Preparation

Clean and rinse the anchovies. Arrange them in a pan. Do not pour any liquid (water or other), nor add any herbs or spices.

Cover the pan and cook for 10-15 minutes, over moderate heat.

Drain the cooked anchovies and season them with a mixture of olive oil, lemon juice, salt and pepper.

Optional ingredients: sardines or mackerels instead of anchovies.

STOCCAFISSO SCOSSO

SHAKEN CODFISH

Ingredients

dried codfish (stockfish) 400-500 g
(first-rate) olive oil 5-8 tbsp
garlic 3-4 cloves
(fresh) parsley
potatoes 1 kg
salt, pepper

Preparation

Soak the dried cod fish in water for 2-4 days, changing the water daily. Then cook the cod fish in fresh water. Clean the cooked fish and cut the meat into pieces.

Cook the (unpeeled) potatoes in water. After that, peel them and cut into slices, not too thin.

Finely chop the parsley leaves and crush the peeled garlic cloves.

In a pot, alternately arrange layers of the sliced cooked potatoes and pieces of the cooked cod. Each potato layer as well as the cod layers season with oil, salt, pepper, parsley and garlic. Cover the pan and hold it in a way that each fist holds a pot handle, but at the same time press the pot cover with your thumbs. Then energetically shake the covered pot, 10-15 times.

eat and love Tuscany

Optional ingredients: green olives, coarsly chopped.

STOCCAFISSO IN UMIDO
CODFISH STEW

Ingredients

dried codfish (stockfish)
400-500 g
tomato paste 1-2 tsp
olive oil 5-8 tbsp
garlic 3-4 cloves
potatoes 2 lb
salt, pepper
parsley

Preparation

Soak the dried cod fish in water for 2-4 days, changing the water daily. Then cut the cod into pieces, removing the bones.

Peel the potatoes and cut them also into pieces, not too small.

Chop finely the parsley and garlic.

In a pot alternately arrange layers of cod and potato pieces. Each layer season with oil, salt, pepper, garlic and parsley. Add the tomato paste, but not much. Pour some water, not as much as to exceed the level of the surface of the ingredients in the pot. Cover the pot and cook over medium heat for 1-1.5 hours. Shake the pot from time to time, but do not stir.

Optional ingredients: bell peppers, leeks, broad beans, peas, mushrooms, pine nuts, raisins.

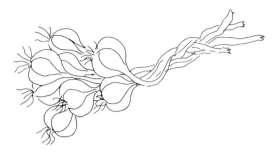

Optional herbs and spices: dry white wine, sweet wine, chili peppers, fried onions, black or green olives, carrots, milk, desalted anchovy fillets, basil, paprika powder, shallots, marjoram, vegetable bouillon powder, celery, capers, cloves, oregano, rosemary, bay leaves, apples, honey, cinnamon, nutmeg, lemon zest and juice, bread crumbs, vinegar, prunes, sugar.

STOCCAFISSO MANTECATO
WHIPPED CODFISH

Ingredients

dried cod fish (stockfish) 600 g
olive oil 1½ - 2 cups
garlic 2-5 cloves
salt, pepper
parsley

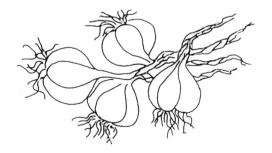

Preparation

Soak the dried cod fish in water for 2-4 days, changing the water daily. Then cook the cod fish in fresh water.

Clean the cooked fish, removing the skin and the bones) and cut the meat into pieces. Then beat the fish meat until it becomes a pulp. Add the parsley and garlic, minced separately. After that, drizzle and stir in the oil. Season with salt and (freshly ground) pepper.

Optional herbs and spices: milk, cinnamon, green olives.

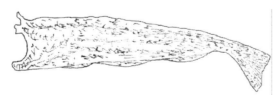

Possible omissions: parsley or garlic.

Suggestions: Serve the whipped stockfish spread on fresh bread slices or with polenta.

TRIGLIE AL SUCCO D'ARANCIA
RED MULLET FISH WITH ORANGE JUICE

Ingredients

red mullets 1 kg
olive oil 4-7 tbsp
oranges 1-2
salt, pepper

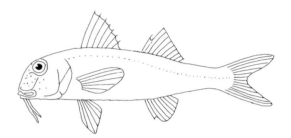

Preparation

Clean and rinse the fish, leaving the heads on.

In a wide pan pour 1-2 tablespoons of oil and then arrange layers of fish, every layer seasoned with salt and orange juice. Do not add water. Cook for 15-20 minutes, over medium heat.

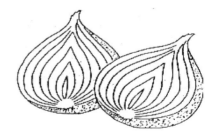

Optional herbs and spices: dry white wine, bread crumbs, fried onions, shallots, thyme, parsley.

SARDINE IMPANATE

SARDINES COATED IN BREAD CRUMBS

Ingredients

(big) sardines 700 g
bread crumbs 100-150 g
flour 50-80 g
eggs 3-4
frying oil
salt

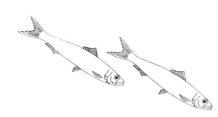

Preparation

Clean and rinse the sardines. Cut off the heads. Using a knife, open the sardines like a book and remove their spines (again using a knife, all along the spine).

Press the sardines into the flour, then dip them in the beaten eggs and finally press them in the bread crumbs to coat. Lay the fried breaded sardines on a paper towel to drain off. Salt and serve.

Optional herbs and spices to add to the beaten eggs: water, milk, vegetable bouillon powder, crushed garlic, chopped parsley, chopped rocket salad, grated cheese, paprika powder, chili pepper, capers, olive oil (especially if the sardines are to be baked in a non-stick pan with no oil or butter, over low heat).

Optional herbs and spices to add to the bread crumbs: garlic, parsley, basil, lemon zest, rosemary, sage, chopped dried tomatoes.

Optional seasonings for the fried breaded sardines: thin lemon slices or lemon juice, finely chopped parsley.

Suggestions: Cutting off the tail, before opening the sardine, facilitates the succeeding process of opening the sardine and the pulling off the spine.

TONNO AL LIMONE

TUNA WITH LEMON SAUCE

Ingredients

fresh raw tuna 1 kg
olive oil 4-5 tbsp
bay leaves 3-4
salt, pepper
celery 1 rib
lemon 1-2
carrots 1
onion 1

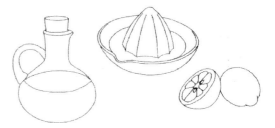

Preparation

Cut the tuna meat into cubes, not too small. Chop the celery and onion. Grate the carrot.

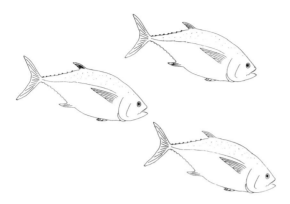

In a pan warm up the oil and fry the onions, celery and carrot, over low heat. After that, put in the tuna meat. Fry over medium heat and then add the bay leaves and lemon juice. Turn the cubes over once. Season with salt and pepper.

Continue cooking on moderate heat, pouring some water from time to time. Do not stir, shake gently the pan.

Optional herbs: black olives.

SEPPIE CON LE FAVE

CUTTLEFISH WITH BROAD BEANS

Ingredients

cuttlefish 300 g
dry white wine 100-150 ml
broad beans 500-700 g
olive oil 4-5 tbsp
garlic 2-3 cloves
salt, pepper
onions 1-2
parsley

Preparation

Clean and rinse the cuttlefish. Cut the cuttlefish into pieces. Chop the garlic and parsley.

In a pan warm up the oil. Fry the onions over low heat. Then add the garlic and parsley. Stir a couple of times and put in the cuttlefish and broad beans. Cook over medium heat for 20-30 minutes.

Optional ingredients: peas, artichokes, tomatoes, potatoes, pancetta (dried bacon), mushrooms, garbanzo beans (chickpeas), beans, lentils.

Optional herbs and spices: saffron, sweet wine, bay leaves, red wine, capers, basil, vegetable bouillon powder.

Optional ingredients at the end: vinegar.

eat and love Tuscany

INSALATA DI SEPPIE

CUTTLEFISH SALAD

Ingredients

cuttlefish 1 kg
olive oil 4-5 tbsp
vinegar 100 ml
salt, pepper
onion 1-2

Preparation

Clean and rinse the cuttlefish. Cook the cuttlefish in water for 20-30 minutes. Cut the cooked cuttlefish into short sticks.

Peel the onions and cut them into thin strips.

In bowl mix the cuttlefish, onions, oil, vinegar, salt and pepper.

Optional ingredients: cooked potatoes, cheese, cooked broad beans or chick peas (garbanzo beans), cooked or grilled squid, cooked octopus.

Optional herbs and spices: garlic, parsley, celery, basil, wild fennel, bay leaves, oregano, capers, black or green olives, tomatoes, rocket salad, pickled gherkins, chives, honey, shallots, lemon zest or juice.

Suggestions: The cuttlefish salad is best served after a couple of hours.

CALAMARI FRITTI

FRIED SQUID

Ingredients

squid (calamari) 1,25 kg
frying oil
lemon 1
flour
salt

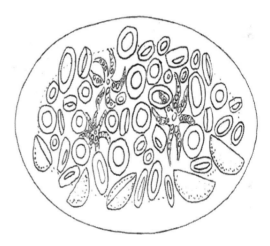

Preparation

Clean and rinse the squid. Drain the squid and then cut it into rings, not too narrow.

Keep the squid in the refrigerator until needed.

Warm up an abbundant quantity of the oil, over high heat. Take the squid out of the refrigerator and promptly proceed. Press the squid rings in flour and fry them (not too many at one time) for a minute over high heat and later on over medium heat. Take them out as soon as they appear to be ready.

Salt the fried squid and serve immediately, with lemon segments or lemon juice.

Optional herbs and spices for the flour: garlic, parsley, paprika powder, corn flour.

Optional seasonings of the fried squid: pepper, mayonnaise, parsley, (white) vinegar, garlic, capers, oregano.

Suggestions: Change the frying oil after no more then three batches.

CALAMARI RIPIENI

STUFFED SQUID

Ingredients

squid (calamari) 800 g
bread crumbs 2-3 tbsp
olive oil 1-2 tbsp
garlic 3-4 cloves
rice 100 g / 3 oz
salt, pepper
parsley
flour

Preparation

Clean and rinse the squid. Chop finely the garlic and parsley. Cook the rice and drain it.

Fry briefly the squid heads and tentacles in some oil. Take them out and drain them. Then finely chop the heads and tentacles. Mix them in a bowl with the parsley, garlic, bread crumbs, rice, salt and pepper.

Use the mixture to fill in the squid mantles. Close the open ends of the mantles and fix them with toothpicks.

Press the stuffed squid mantles in the flour. Fry them in some oil (not much).

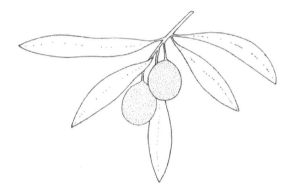

Optional ingredients of the filling: scampi or shrimp tail meat, clam or mussel meat, cooked cuttlefish, fried mushrooms, pancetta (dried bacon), mortadella, cooked egg yolks, beaten eggs, (raw o fried) fish meat, ham, prosciutto ham, mashed cooked potatoes, canned tuna meat, cheese, ricotta cheese, fried zucchini, leeks, cooked peas, cooked broad beans, (dried) tomatoes, black or green olives, soft inside of a bread slice (soaked in milk or water and drained afterwards), figs, ground almonds, cooked barley, raisins (soaked and drained), (gently fried) pine nuts.

Optional herbs and spices of the filling: oregano, celery, lemon zest and juice, desalted anchovy fillets, tomato paste, basil, vegetable bouillon powder, rosemary, saffron, squid ink, nutmeg, cream, dry white wine, vinegar, sage, wild fennel, fried onions, green onions, capers, mint, chives.

Optional ingredients at the end: lemon juice, lemon slices, parsley, garlic, olive oil.

Possible omissions: rice, garlic.

Optional proceeding: Pour some wine (two or three tablespoons) 2-3 times during the frying process.

Different method: Bake the stuffed squid in an oven or grill them.

POLPO AL FORNO

BAKED OCTOPUS

Ingredients

octopus, 2-3 smaller ones, 1.5-2 kg
potatoes 1-1.5 kg
olive oil 4-5 tbsp
salt, pepper

Preparation

Clean the octopuses, rinse them and cut them into pieces. Peel the potatoes and slice them.

In a baking pan lay the potatoes and over them arrange a layer of octopus cuts. Season with oil, salt and pepper.

Put the pan in a preheated oven and bake for app. an hour at a medium high temperature.

Optional ingredients: (red) bell peppers, zucchini, tomatoes, eggplants.

Optional herbs and spices: garlic, parsley, rosemary, dry white wine, (red) onions, green onions, bay leaves, carrots, shallots, green or black olives, lemon zest and juice, chili peppers, capers, sage, vegetable bouillon powder, paprika powder, apple, fresh figs, sweet wine.

Optional proceeding: Cover the baking pan.

BUSARA

Ingredients

clams or mussels 1.5-2 kg
or
scampi 1 kg
brandy (cognac, armagnac) 1-3 tbsp
dry white wine 100-200 ml
bread crumbs 2-3 tbsp
tomato paste 1 tsp
olive oil 5-6 tbsp
garlic 2-4 cloves
salt, pepper
parsley

Preparation

Clean and rinse the clams, mussels or

scampi. Chop finely the garlic and parsley.

In a large pan warm up the oil. Fry briefly the garlic and parsley, over low heat. Then stir in the bread crumbs. Continue stirring for a minute or two and after that put in the clams, mussels or scampi. Stir for a minute. Pour in the wine and stir in the tomato paste. Let the wine partly evaporate.

Continue cooking for another 10-15 minutes, pouring in some water, when needed. Stir from time to time. In the end, season with salt, pepper and cognac.

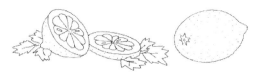

Optional herbs and spices: lemon zest and juice, vegetable bouillon powder, chili pepper, paprika powder, celery, sweet wine, mint, sugar, green olives, oregano, saffron, bay leaves, pine nuts, ground almonds, shallots, onions, cream.

GRILLED BRANZINI

Ingredients

bass (spigola, branzino) 2-4
(1-1,25 kg)
olive oil 4-5 tbsp
lemons 2-3
basil
salt

Preparation

Clean the fish, leaving the head on.

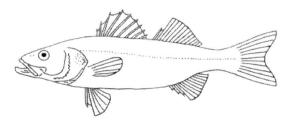

Season the inside of the fish with a mix of lemon zest and juice. Then oil the outside of the fish and season with salt. Grill the fish using a grill or a grill pan. Season the grilled fish with some olive oil.

Optional herbs and spices: garlic, rosemary.

BOTTARGA DI ORBETELLO

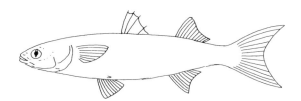

The bottarga from Orbetello is obtained from the ovarian sac of the Mugil Cephalus mullet, which is extracted manually, then salted, washed, dried and stored under vacuum.

In Orbetello the bottarga has been produced for centuries.

The bottarga is excellent as an appetizer seasoned with extra virgin olive oil, pepper and lemon, or as a condiment for pasta.

TONNO UBRIACO

DRUNKEN TUNA

Ingredients

tuna fish (four slices) 500-700 g
red wine 150-200 ml
olive oil 4-5 tbsp
garlic 1-2 cloves
salt, pepper
onion 1
parsley
flour

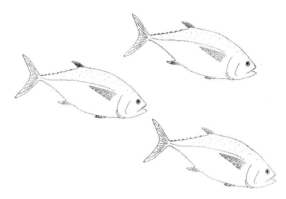

Preparation

Peel and chop the onion, crush the peeled garlic. Fry the onion gently in a some oil. When the onion is well co- lored, add the garlic, stir a few times and then place the slices of floured tuna. Add salt and pepper to taste and brown the fish, both sides, and then pour the red wine over it.

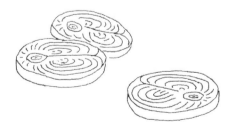

Cook for another 10 minutes over medium heat.

BACCALÀ ALLA FIORENTINA

COD, THE FLORENCE WAY

Ingredients

salted cod fish 600-800 g
fresh tomatoes or tomato passata 400-600 g
olive oil 5-6 tbsp onion 1
garlic 2-4 cloves
salt, pepper
rosemary
parsley
flour

Preparation

Soak the salted cod fish in water for 1-2 days, changing the water daily.

In a casserole gently fry the onion cut into thin slices, adding later even the crushed garlic cloves and chopped rosemary. Stir a few times and then add the tomatoes, salt and pepper and keep on cooking over low heat.

Meanwhile, take the cod, remove the skin and bones, then rinse and dry well. Cut the fillets into pieces, not too small, and then flour them.

Fry the pieces of floured fish and pla- ce them to cool on absorbent paper.

Put the pieces of fried cod into the tomato sauce, in a single layer, and let it cook for 5-6 minutes Then turn off the heat and sprinkle with plenty of freshly ground black pepper and chopped parsley.

Optional ingredients: onion, sugar, potatoes, green or black olives, peas, celery, dry white wine, basil, pine nuts, raisins.

ACCIUGHE ALLA POVERA

Ingredients

very fresh anchovies 500 g
white wine vinegar 200 ml
white onions 2-3
olive oil 6-7 tbsp
lemon 1

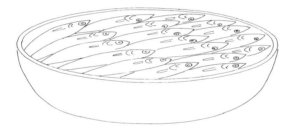

Preparation

Clean the anchovies and extract the fillets. Peel the onions and slice them thinly.

Put the fillets in a bowl. On each layer, arrange the onion slices and sprinkle with lemon juice and vinegar. Leave the anchovies marinated in the fridge for 1-2 hours.

Drain the anchovies from the marinade, sprinkle them with abundant olive oil and let them rest for at least 7-8 hours before serving them.

Tips: Serve the marinated anchovies with the freshly sliced white onion.

Optional spices and herbs: salt, pepper, peperoncino (chili pepper).

SARDE IN DOLCEFORTE

Ingredients

sardines 1 kg
white wine vinegar
or
lemon juice
150-200 ml
pine nuts 3-4 tbsp
olive oil 2-3 tbsp
white onion 2-3
raisins 3-4 tbsp
salt, pepper
frying oil

Preparation

Clean the sardines and open them like a book. Rinse them, drain and then roll them in flour. After that fry them in oil.

Place the fried sardines in layers in a bowl, adding the raisins and pine nuts to each layer.

In a pan, cook the sliced onions, with vinegar and some olive oil, salt and pepper, over a medium heat.

A few minutes later, pour the onion and the sauce over the sardines.

Let the seasoned sardins rest until tomorrow, before ser-ving them.

Optional ingredients of the sauce: rosemary, garlic, fried shrimp, peperoncino (chili pepper).

CAZZALÀ

Type of polenta, not too thick, seasoned with meat or mushroom sauce.

MATALUFFI

The mataluffi differs from the cazzalà because the polenta is seasoned with olive oil and grated cheese.

PESCE AZZURO IN SALSA DI CAPPERI

BLUE FISH WITH CAPER SAUCE

Ingredients

sardines, mackerel, tuna 1 kg
olive oil 5-6 tbsp
capers 1-3 tbsp
salt, pepper
lemon 2
vinegar
parsley

Preparation

Blanch the blue fish in salted water acidulated with about 25% vinegar for a few minutes (depending on the weight). The water should just cover the fish. Let the fish cool and then remove the bones.

Place the fish fillets on a serving dish and lightly pepper them. Prepare a limon sauce emulsifying the oil with the lemon and salt, add the chopped capers and parsley and spread the sauce over the fish.

ORATA AL VINO

GILTHEAD IN WINE SAUCE

Ingredients

gilthead 1-1.25 kg
dry white wine 200-250 ml
olive oil 5-6 tbsp
garlic 1-2 cloves
salt, pepper
onion 1
parsley

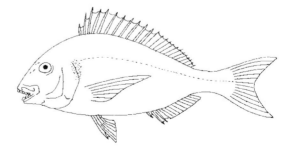

Preparation

After cleaning the gilthead, place it on a well-oiled baking sheet. Cover it with chopped onion and garlic, pour over the wine and some olive oil. Season with salt and pepper. Bake at 160 degrees.

ACCIUGATA DEL VALDARNO

Ingredients

salted anchovie fillets 20-30
olive oil 8-10 tbsp
capers 4-5 tbsp

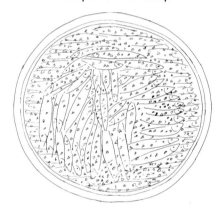

Preparation

In a saucepan, in olive oil, over low heat, slowly dissolve the salted anchovies fillets. Mix in the finely chopped capers.

Let the sauce rest for a minute or two and then serve it with toasted bread or otherwise.

ACCIUGHE SOTTO PESTO

Ingredients

salted anchovies fillets 20-30
olive oil 7-10 tbsp
garlic 1-3 cloves
parsley

Preparation

In a bowl, alternate a layer of anchovie fillets, chopped parsley and plenty of extra virgin olive oil, making several layers until all the ingredients are used up. Let the seasoned anchovies flavor for at least an hour and then serve them with (toasted or fresh) bread spread with garlic, butter or mascarpone.

Additional ingredients: peperoncino (chili pepper), capers, vinegar.

ACCIUGHE CON CIPOLLINE

Ingredients

salted anchovies fillets 20-30
spring onions 5-7
or
onions 1-2
olive oil 7-10 tbsp
vinegar 2-5 tbsp

Preparation

Place the anchovie fillets in a serving plate. Slice the onions thinly and spread them over the anchovies. Season with the olive oil and vinegar, maybe also chili peppers or capers.

eat and love Tuscany

VEGETABLES

FAGIOLINI AL POMODORO

Ingredients

green beans 500 g
tomatoes 250-350 g
olive oil 4-5 tbsp
garlic 1-2 cloves
chili pepper 1
onion 1
basil
salt

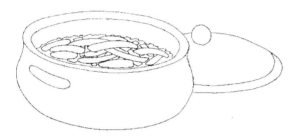

Preparation

Pour some oil in a pan. Fry gently the finely chopped onion and garlic over low heat. Add the tomatoes cut into small pieces and the chopped chilli. Stir and cook for several minutes. Then add the chopped green beans and basil.

Continue cooking for half an hour, stirring occasionally and pouring in some water, if necessary.

Optional additions: potatoes, oregano, celery, bacon, sugar.

PATATE ALLA CONTADINA

POTATOES, THE FARMERS WAY

Ingredients

potatoes 1 kg
olive oil 5-6 tbsp
salt, pepper
rosemary
sage

Preparation

Peel, wash, drain and then cut the potatoes into small pieces, but not too small.

Heat the oil with rosemary and sage. Put the potatoes in and add the salt and pepper. Cook over medium heat, stirring very often.

PANZANELLA TOSCANA

Ingredients

slices of yesterday's bread 4-5
ripe tomatoes 3-4
olive oil 5-6 tbsp
red onion 1-2
wine vinegar
salt, pepper
basil

Preparation

Slice the onions thinly. Transfer it into a bowl and let it soak in water with a little vinegar, for 2-3 hours. Then drain the onions.

Peel the tomatoes and cut them into small pieces. Chop the basil.

Cut the bread into thick slices. With a knife, cut the rind off the slices. Soften each slice of bread by wetting it briefly with some water, previously acidulated with a couple of tablespoons of vinegar.

Put the softened bread in a bowl, crumbling it coarsely with your hands. Add the drained onions, chopped tomatoes, chopped basil, oil, pepper and salt. Gently mix all the ingredients.

Let the panzanella rest in the refrigerator for at least an hour. Remove it from the refrigerator 20-30 minutes before serving. Taste the panzanella and add a little vinegar or oil, if necessary.

Optional ingredients: cucumbers, peeled and cut into thin slices, spring onions instead of onions, diced mozzarella, salad.

Optional spices and herbs: oregano, celery.

Panzanella del prete

Panzanella of the priest, appreciated in Garfagnana, includes the addition of boiled eggs, salted anchovies, raw or cooked ham, cheese, carrots, capers, radicchio, fennel, tuna in oil.

Panzanella con tonno e capperi

The recipe for this panzanella besides tuna fish and capers includes the ingredients such as tomato sauce and basil.

SGABEI

Sgabei, pieces of leavened bread dough, fried and salted on the surface, traditionally eaten plain or stuffed with cheese or cold cuts. This dish is typical of Lunigiana.

PASTA E FAGIOLI

Pasta and beans is a typical Italian dish of which there are several regional variations.

The recipe is simple. All the ingredients are put to cook together in water.

Only the (short) pasta is added 5-6 minutes before the end.

Note: Besides the beans, ingredients can typically include olive oil, salt, pepper, garlic, lard, celery, and, depending on the variants, rosemary, thyme, parsley, tomatoes, marjoram, ham, pancetta or pork rind.

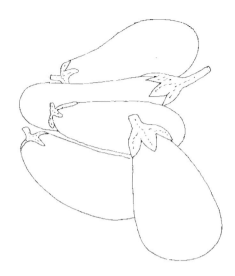

TUSCAN COCCOLI

Ingredients

white flour 500 g
water, skimmed milk
or vegetable broth
400-500 ml
olive oil, butter or lard 3-5 tbsp
brewer's yeast 40-50 g
frying oil
salt

Preparation

Dissolve the yeast in a little of the liquid and then pour it in the center of the flour. Add the fat, salt and remaining liquid (a little at a time), kneading the dough. Cover the dough with a cloth and let it rest for a couple of hours.

Once the time has elapsed, cut the dough in pieces and form balls or cylinders. Fry them in abundant hot oil.

Note: The coccoli are Tuscan savory fritters. Tuscans eat them accompanied by cured ham cut into very thin slices and cheese (stracchino or al.).

Preparation

Clean and rinse the eggplants. Without peeling them, cut the eggplants into small cubes. Sprinkle them with some salt and allow the eggplants to rest salted for half an hour, or an hour, to loose the bitter juices. Then rinse the eggplants and drain them off.

Clean the bell peppers and cut them into pieces. Peel the tomatoes and cut them too. Peel the potatoes and slice them. Chop finely the onions, basil and celery.

CIAMBOTTA

Ingredients

yellow bell pepper 1
ripe tomatoes 2-5
red bell pepper 1
olive oil 4-5 tbsp
celery 1-3 ribs
eggplants 1-2
potatoes 1-2
salt, pepper
onions 1-2
basil

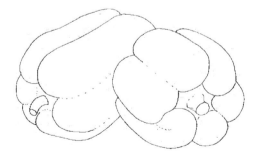

In a pan warm up the oil. Fry the onions over low heat. After that, add all the other vegetables. Cook for 5-6 minutes over medium heat, stirring often. Then season with salt and pepper and pour in the water, as much as is needed to barely cover the ingredients. Continue cooking for 30-45 minutes over moderate heat. Stir every now and then, pouring in some water, not much, when needed.

Optional ingredients: zucchini, black or green olives.

Optional herbs and spices: vegetable bouillon powder, garlic, oregano, parsley, capers, sugar, vinegar.

Optional ingredients at the end: eggs.

Note: This dish is also known as ciammotta or cianfotta.

CARCIOFI RIPIENI
STUFFED ARTICHOKES

Ingredients

artichokes 8-12
ingredients of the selected filling
ripe tomatoes 100-400 g
olive oil 4-5 tbsp
sale, pepe
onion 1

Preparation

Wash the artichokes, drain them off and proceed with the trimming.

Cut off the top of the artichokes, using a knife. Eliminate the outer leaves which are too "woody". Cut off also the sharp points from some of the remaining leaves, this time using kitchen scissors. Then place the artichokes in water with lemon juice in it. Let them soak for 10-15 minutes.

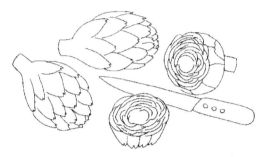

After the soaking, drain them off well. Then open the artichoke leaves, pushing them outside.

Stuff the "blossomed" artichokes with the selected filling.

Peel the tomatoes and cut them into pieces. Chop the onions.

In a wide pan warm up the oil. Fry the onions over low heat. Then add the tomatoes. Lay the stuffed artichokes in the pan, spatter some oil and pour some water.

Cover the pan and cook over low or moderate heat for 20-30 minutes.

Garlic and parsley filling

Prepare a mixture of finely chopped parsley, garlic, bread crumbs, salt and pepper.

Meat filling

Prepare a mixture of ground meat, bread crumbs, egg(s), grated cheese, parsley, salt and pepper.

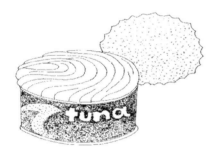

Tuna fish filling

Prepare a mixture of canned tuna, desalted anchovy fillets, capers, garlic, parsley, salt and pepper.

Desalted anchovy filling

Prepare a mixture of desalted anchovy fillets, bread crumbs, garlic, marjoram, parsley, raisins, olive oil, pine nuts and grated cheese.

Caper filling

Prepare a mixture of desalted capers, bread crumbs (slightly toasted in some oil), desalted anchovy fillets, garlic and parsley.

Optional ingredients of the filling: marjoram, pancetta (dried bacon), ham, prosciutto ham, mortadella, grated cheese, soft inside of a bread slice, soaked in milk and then squeezed out, scampi or shrimp tail meat, eggs, cooked egg yolks, whole cooked eggs, ground meat, thyme, wild fennel, vegetable bouillon powder, mint, rosemary, paprika powder, orange juice, dry white wine, bay leaves, capers.

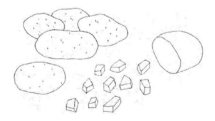

Optional herbs and spices of the sauce: dry white wine, vegetable bouillon powder, balsamic vinegar (aceto balsamico), paprika powder, grated cheese, desalted anchovy fillets.

Optional proceeding: Put the broad beans, peas, potatoes, meat (cut or ground), squid or cuttlefish (cut into pieces) amongst the artichokes, before the beginning of cooking.

CECI LESSATI

COOKED GARBANZO BEANS

(COOKED CHICKPEAS)

Ingredients

garbanzo beans (chickpeas) 500 g
olive oil 6-7 tbsp
salt, pepper

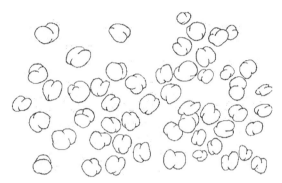

Preparation

Let the garbanzo beans soak, in (warm) water, for 12-24 hours.

Cook the garbanzo beans in water with some oil and salt, over moderate heat.

At the end, season with pepper. Add more salt and oil, if needed.

Optional ingredients: potatoes, barley.

Optional herbs and spices: sage, rosemary, celery, bay leaves, garlic, onions, vegetable bouillon powder, pancetta (dried bacon), leeks.

Optional ingredients at the end: parsley, garlic, thyme, canned tuna fish, anchovy fillets, paprika powder, chili peppers, tomato paste, lemon zest and juice, vinegar, sausages.

PRATAIOLI IMPANATI

MUSHROOMS COATED IN BREAD CRUMBS

Ingredients

white button mushrooms
(champignon) 500 g
bread crumbs
frying oil
eggs 3
flour
salt

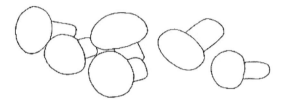

Preparation

Clean the mushrooms and separate the caps from the stalks. Press them in the flour, then in the beaten eggs and then in the crumbs to coat.

Fry the coated mushrooms in an abbundant quantity of frying oil, over medium heat. Remove the fried mushrooms from the oil and put them on paper towels to drain off.

Optional herbs and spices for the beaten eggs: vegetable bouillon powder, grated cheese, parsley, oregano, thyme, basil, cream.

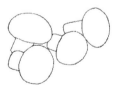

Optional ingredients at the end: mayonnaise, lemon juice.

PEPERONI RIPIENI STUFATI

STUFFED BELL PEPPERS

Ingredients

green bell peppers (or red or yellow)
8 pieces
ripe tomatoes 350-600 g
bread crumbs 1-2 tsp
olive oil 4-5 tbsp
salt, peppers

meat filling:

ground (baby) beef meat 400-500 g
ground pork meat 250-400 g
vegetable bouillon powder
garlic 2-4 cloves
salt, pepper
onions 1-2
eggs 1-2
parsley

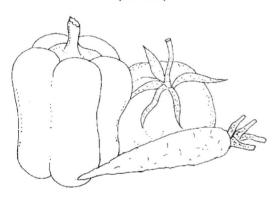

Preparation

Cut off the top of the bell peppers and remove the seeds from the inside. Then wash them and let them drain off.

Chop the onions, garlic and parsley. Peel the tomatoes and cut them into pieces.

In a pan warm up the oil. Fry the onions over low heat. Put in the meat and stir a couple of times. Let the meat fry over medium heat, until the liquid almost evaporates. Then remove the pan from the heat and let the meat cool down.

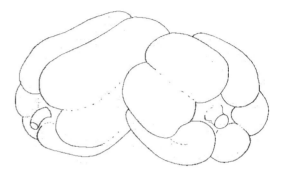

Stir the eggs, garlic and parsley in the meat and then also the vegetable bouillon powder, salt and pepper.

Stuff the peppers with the prepared meat filling.

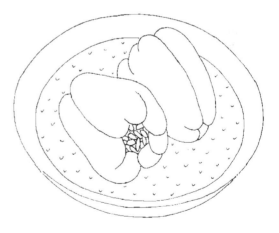

Arrange the stuffed peppers in a wide pot. Add the tomatoes and pour some water, enough to reach to the 4/5 of the level of the peppers.

Season with salt and pepper. Cover the pot and cook over moderate heat. Agitate the pot every now and then.

Minutes before removing the pot from the heat, add some bread crumbs, but not much.

Optional ingredients of the filling: other types of meat, rice, pancetta (dried bacon), mashed cooked potatoes, grated raw potatoes, cooked eggs, bread crumbs, mushrooms, black or green olives, pasta cooked very much "al dente", cheese, ricotta cheese, grated cheese, fresh cheese, cream, sour cream, paprika powder, soft inside of eggplants or zucchini, tomato paste, basil, capers, nutmeg, wild fennel, chili peppers, celery, rosemary, oregano, chives, carrots, mint, desalted anchovy fillets, pine nuts, soft inside of a bread slice, soaked in water or milk, and then squeezed out, canned tuna fish instead of meat, raisins.

Optional herbs and spices for the sauce: bay leaves, garlic, vegetable bouillon powder, grated carrots, parsley, celery, vinegar.

Optional ingredients at the end: cream, sour cream, grated cheese.

Possible omissions: beef meat.

Different method: Bake the stuffed peppers in an oven.

PEPERONATA

Ingredients

green, red and yellow bell peppers 800 g
ripe tomatoes 300-400 g
olive oil 4-5 tbsp
garlic 1-3 cloves
onions 1-2
parsley
salt

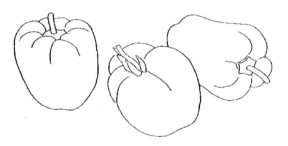

Preparation

Seed the bell peppers and cut them into short and narrow sticks. Peel the tomatoes and cut them into pieces. Peel the onions and the garlic and chop them finely.

In a pan warm up the oil. Fry the onions over low heat. Soon add the garlic. Then put in the bell peppers and continue cooking for 5-6 minutes, over medium heat. After that add the tomatoes. Cook for half an hour, still over medium heat. Stir from time to time, pouring in some water when necessary. Minutes before the end of the cooking, season the dish with the parsley and salt.

Optional ingredients: eggplants, zucchini, potatoes, olives, rice, sausages, pancetta (dried bacon).

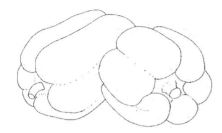

Optional herbs and spices: basil, oregano, bay leaves, vinegar, dry white wine, marjoram, thyme, mint, capers, desalted anchovy fillets.

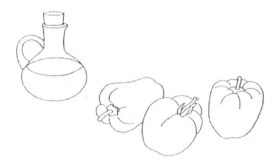

Optional ingredients at the end: grated cheese, paprika powder, vinegar.

PISELLI IN UMIDO
PEA STEW

Ingredients

peas 700 g
pancetta (dried bacon) 100-200 g
tomato paste 1 tsp
olive oil 4-5 tbsp
garlic 2-3 tbsp
salt, pepper
onions 1-2
parsley

Preparation

Cut the pancetta (dried bacon) into small cubes. Finely chop the onions, garlic and parsley.

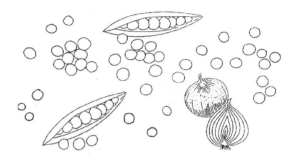

Warm up the oil in a pan. Fry the pancetta, onions, garlic and parsley, over low heat, stirring often. After a few minutes, add the peas and stir in the tomato paste. Cook for another 15-20 minutes over medium heat. Season with salt and pepper.

Optional ingredients: potatoes, (ground) meat, mushrooms, broad beans, garbanzo beans (already cooked).

Optional herbs and spices: vegetable bouillon powder, carrots, thyme, bay leaves, wild fennel, mint, basil, sugar, nutmeg, cloves, capers, dry white wine, red wine, saffron, cream.

Optional ingredients at the end: grated cheese, nutmeg.

Possible omissions: onions, tomatoes.

ZUCCHINE IMPANATE
ZUCCHINI
COATED IN BREAD CRUMBS

Ingredients

zucchini 600 g
bread crumbs
salt, pepper
eggs 2-3
frying oil
flour

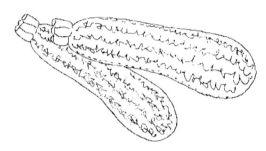

Preparation

Cut the zucchini into slices, not too thin. Press the zucchini slices in the flour, then in the beaten eggs and finally in the crumbs to coat.

Fry the coated zucchini slices in an abbundant quantity of oil. The fried slices put on kitchen paper towels to drain off.

Optional herbs and spices for the beaten eggs: vegetable bouillon powder, grated cheese, cream, milk.

Optional ingredients at the end: sugar, lemon juice.

PATATE ALLA CONTADINA
POTATOES, PEASENT STYLE

Ingredients

potatoes 1 kg
pancetta 100-150 g
olive oil 5-6 tbsp
salt, pepper
onion 1
sage

Preparation

Peel and rinse the potatoes. Cut them into pieces, not too small.

Warm up the oil in a pan. Put in the potatoes, chopped pancetta, onion and sage, salt and pepper. Cook over medium heat, stirring very often.

Optional herbs and spices: marjoram, tomato paste, garlic, parsley.

PARMIGIANA DI MELANZANE

EGGPLANT PARMIGIANA

Ingredients

eggplants 1 kg
caciocavallo cheese 200 g
grated cheese 100 g
olive oil 5-6 tbsp
onion 1 (small)
tomatoes 1 kg
garlic 2 cloves
basil
salt

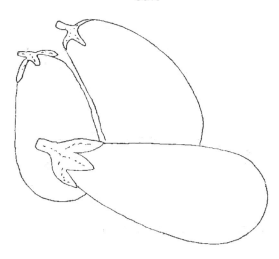

Preparation

With the tomatoes and oil prepare a tomato sauce.

Remove the sauce from the heat and stir in the chopped basil and salt.

Peel the eggplants and cut them into slices, not too thin. Sprinkle them with salt and let them rest for at least

half an hour, to release the bitter juices. Then rinse and drain them off.

Press the eggplant slices into flour and then fry them in some oil. Put the fried eggplant slices on kitchen paper towels to drain them off.

Pour one half of the tomato sauce into a baking oven. Then lay the eggplant slices in the sauce and cover them with the remaining tomato sauce. Sprinkle with grated cheese and lay over the caciocavalo cheese slices.

Repeat the procedure until all the ingredients are exhausted.

Bake the "parmigiana" for 30-40 minutes at a moderate temperature.

Optional ingredients: zucchini slices, cooked eggs, mozzarella cheese instead of caciocavallo.

Optional proceeding: Grill the eggplants slices instead of frying them.

INSALATA DI PATATE

POTATO SALAD

Ingredients

potatoes 0.7-1 kg
pickled bell peppers 12-4 tbsp
desalted anchovy fillets 4-5
pickled onions 50-100 g
white vinegar 1 tbsp
pickled gherkins 4-6
olive oil 3-4 tbsp
desalted capers
mustard ½ tsp
boiled egg 1
salt, pepper

Preparation

Dice and slice the boiled potatoes and

mix them with all the other ingredients.

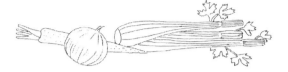

Optional ingredients: back or green olives, canned tuna, canned artichokes, canned mushrooms.

SPINACI ALLA FIORENTINA

Ingredients

spinach 1 kg
grated cheese 60 g
olive oil 3-4 tbsp
garlic 1-2 cloves
milk 200 ml
salt, pepper
butter 20 g
flour 20 g
nutmeg

Preparation

Peel the spinach leaves, removing the stems, and wash them. Boil them in water. Drain them, squeeze them and then chop them.

Pour the spinach in a pan and let it dry over a moderate heat. Add the finely chopped garlic. Stir often.

Prepare a béchamel using milk, flour and butter. Then add the grated cheese, nutmeg, salt and pepper.

Mix the spinach with one half of the bechamel and pour it in an oiled baking pan. Cover it with the remaining béchamel and put the pan in the oven.

Gratinate at 180-200 ° until the surface becomes golden.

FAGIOLI ALL'UCCELLETTO

Ingredients

fresh white beans
(cannellini, toscanelli, caponi) 600 g
or
soaked dried beans 300 g
ripe tomatoes 100-300 g
olive oil 4-5 tbsp
garlic 2-3 cloves
salt and pepper
sage

Preparation

Put the beans in lightly salted cold water. Bring to a boil and cook over moderate heat. Drain the boiled beans.

Heat the oil in a saucepan. Put the finely chopped garlic and sage. Stir a few times and add the still hot beans. Stir for 4-5 minutes over medium heat.

Meanwhile peel the tomatoes and cut them into small pieces. Add them to the beans and continue cooking for another 10-20 minutes, over moderate heat. Season with salt and pepper.

Optional spices and herbs: garlic, celery, rosemary, bay leaves, chilli, sugar, oregano, sausages, onion, tomato sauce, tomato passata, sage.

Note: Typical dish of Tuscan cuisine, especially of Florence.

FOCACCIA SERAVEZZINA

Ingredients

white flour (whole) 250 g
black olives 70-120 g
olive oil 2-3 tbsp
corn flour 150 g
garlic 1-2 cloves
yeast 1 sachet
lard 50-60 g
rosemary
salt

Preparation

Mix all the ingredients well: the two flours, the yeast, the salt, the oil, the olives, the lard, and the chopped rosemary, the crushed garlic and the water.

Let the dough rest for 30 minutes.

Then roll out the dough into a 1.5-3 cm thick sheet. Place it in a greased baking pan. Lightly salt the surface and sprinkle with a few drops of oil.

Let the focaccia rise again for another 3 minutes.

After this, bake the focaccia at 200-220 ° C for 25-40 minutes.

Let the baked focaccia rest a little and then serve it.

Optional ingredients: raisins, basil, pine nuts.

Suggestions: Serve the focaccia with cheese or salami.

Note: The focaccia di Seravezza is also called marocca or morocco bread.

SCARPACCIA SALATA CON ZUCCHINE

Ingredients

olive oil 2-3 tbsp
bread crumbs
flour 70-80 g
zucchini 3-4
milk 100 ml
yeast 5 g
egg 1
basil
salt

Preparation

On a cutting board, thinly slice the zucchini.

In a bowl, mix well the egg and the milk. Then add the flour, salt and a teaspoon of instant yeast. After that, also add the thinly sliced zucchini.

Transfer everything into a 24 cm diameter baking pan covered with parchment paper. Sprinkle with some breadcrumbs. Bake at 160 ° C for about an hour, until it is browned.

Note: The scarpaccia is a traditional dish from the city of Camaiore in Tuscany.

Optional ingredients: The scarpaccia can be prepared with various vegetables.

Note: A sweet version of scarpaccia also exists, the scarpaccia viareggina, also a vegetable cake, that is typical of the Viareggio area.

GLI GNUDI
(ravioli gnudi alla fiorentina, malfatti)

Ingredients

fresh (or frozen) spinach 300-600 g
grated cheese 150-200 g
sheep ricotta 400-500 g
salt, pepper
flour q.b.
eggs 3-5
nutmeg

Preparation

Boil the spinach for 3-4 minutes in plenty of salted water. Then drain it well and let it cool. After that squeeze the spinach, draining it once more. Chop the boiled spinach coarsely.

In a bowl mix the spinach, ricotta (adding it part by part), flour, grated cheese, eggs, nutmeg, salt and pepper.

Shape the mixture into balls of 4-5 cm. Pass the balls in the flour. Boil in plenty of salted water and when it reaches a simmer, put in the gnudi ravioli, a few at a time. Cook them for 2-3 minutes, until they start to float. Then drain them and season them with melted butter and grated cheese. Serve them right away, still quite warm.

The gnudi can be served with a light tomato sauce or simply with butter and sage.

Suggestions: Gnudi you can finish au gratin with bechamel or seasoned with butter and sage or with tomato sauce and basil.

Optional procedure: Lightly fry the boiled and squeezed spinach with oil and garlic, before further use.

Different preparation: Cook the gnudi in oven for 10-15 minutes at 180 ° C.

Note: Typical dish of Tuscan cuisine. The gnudi are gnocchetti made from flour, spinach, chard or other vegetables, ricotta, grated cheese, spices and sometimes even eggs, floured and boiled in water.

These gnocchetti are widespread in the Tuscan region, especially in Val di Chiana and in the Casentino area.

The term "ravioli gnudi" derives from the fact that these ravioli are not covered by pasta, they are "nude".

Although not really a pasta format, the gnudi are one of the most popular first courses in the region.

POMODORI ALLA MUGELLANA

Ingredients

tomatoes 3-4
vegetable bouillon powder
olive oil 5-6 tbsp
garlic 3-4 cloves
salt, pepper
parsley
flour

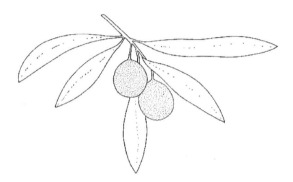

Preparation

Cut the tomatoes into slices and flour them.

Gently fry a mixture of crushed garlic and minced parsley, in some olive oil, over moderate heat.

Add the tomatoes and the vegetable bouillon powder. Cook for 15-20 minutes, over medium heat, season with salt and pepper, and serve the tomatoes on toasted bread or otherwise.

PITONCA

The pitonca is a type of polenta, with a rather complex preparation procedure.

Before joining the corn flour, a considerable number of ingredients are used: celery, carrots, leeks, potatoes, beans, black cabbage, tomato sauce and lard.

The pitonca is served after boiling, seasoning and frying.

FAVE AI POMODORI

Ingredients

fresh young broad beans in pods 1 lg
tomato passata 100-200 ml
peperoncino (chili pepper)
olive oil 4-5 tbsp
spring onion 1-3
garlic 1-2 cloves
salt, pepper
parsley

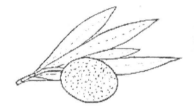

Preparation

Peel the broad beans and boil them. Cut the pods into pieces and blanch them for about 15-20 minutes in salted water. After that drain them.

In a non-stick pan, brown the finely sliced onions with a pinch of peperoncino. Add the broad beans, pods, tomatoes, parsley and salt. Cook them over medium heat for about 5-10 minutes.

Note: Instead of the broad beans, the fresh peas can be used.

FRITTATA
DI
ASPARAGI SELVATICI

Boil the asparagus, only for a minute or two. Drain the asparagus and then fry them in some olive oil. Soon add the beaten eggs and season with salt.

FRITTATA
DI
PORCINI MUSHROOMS

Slice the porcini mushrooms. Fry the mushrooms in some olive oil, seasoned with salt. When the liquid is almost evaporated, add the beaten eggs.

FRITTATA
IN
TRIPPA
(FINTA TRIPPA)

Beat a couple of eggs, with some salt.

In a pan, over very low heat, brown some breadcrumbs and grated cheese. Pour in the beaten eggs and fry for a couple minutes over moderate heat. Then remove the frittata from the pan and cut it in short spaghetti-like strips.

Prepare or warm up the tomato sauce. rather thick. Add and stir in the frittata strips.

SFORMATO
DI
FINOCCHI

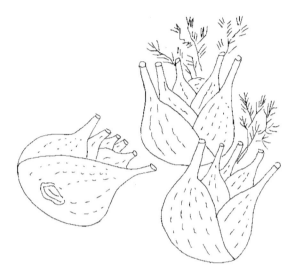

Clean the fennels and boil them in abundant salted water. Once cooked, drain and chop them, place them in a bowl and add the béchamel, nutmeg, salt, pepper, oil and grated cheese.

Butter or oil the baking pan and sprinkle it with breadcrumbs. Put in and spread the previously prepared mixture and bake at 180 ° for about 30 minutes.

MELANZANE
SOTTO IL PESTO

Slice the aubergines lengthwise.

Prepare a pesto, a mixture of crushed garlic and chili peppers, with olive oil, vinegar and salt.

Fry the aubergine slices in some olive oil.

Place the fried aubergine slices in a bowl, seasoning them with the prepared pesto.

Let the seasoned aubergines rest for a couple of hours and then serve them.

ZUCCHINI IN TRIPPA
(zucchini trippati)

Ingredients

zucchini 4-8
peperoncino (chili pepper)
grated cheese 50-100 g
olive oil 4-5 tbsp
garlic 1-3 cloves
tomatoes 2-3
salt, pepper

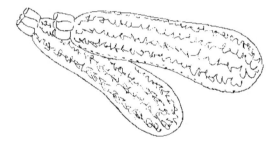

Preparation

Wash and remove the zucchini tops. Cut them lengthwise into four segments. Then cut each segment into strips.

In a pan, in some oil, fry gently the crushed garlic and chili pepper. Add the zucchini and fry them, stirring frequently. After a couple of minutes, add the tomatoes, already cut into small pieces. Season with salt and pepper. Finish cooking and serve.

When served, or a minute before, generously sprinkle with grated cheese, maybe even with some breadcrumbs.

IL FAGIOLO DI SORANA

In the area that goes from Sorana to Castelvecchio, in Tuscany, there is a micro-area that allows the optimal cultivation of the Fagiolo di Sorana.

This type of bean is very small, very light, of a beautiful natural white color. The thin skin and delicate taste make it a highly sought after product.

FAGIOLI NEL FIASCO

Ingredients

small white beans
(fagioli di Sorana, zolfini, toscanelli o cannellini)
500 g
olive oil 5-6 tbsp
garlic 1-2 cloves
sage 3-7 leaves
salt, pepper

Preparation

Soak the beans for 12 hours in cold water.

After that drain the beans and put them in a bottle or in a flask (preferably with a large opening), or a suitable pot, together with the oil, garlic, sage, some peppercorns and a pinch of salt.

Pour in enough water to cover the beans by a centimeter or two. Dip the flask in a pot full of water, in fact on a clean cloth, folded several times, already placed on the bottom. Cook for about 3-5 hours, in fact as long as it takes for the liquid in the bean flask to almost evaporate.

Do not add water to the beans, but only to the water bath, keeping the level more or less constant. When the beans are cooked, turn off the heat, let them rest for 15 minutes and then transfer them to the serving dish.

Season the beans, cooked in tuscan bain-marie manner, with olive oil and freshly ground pepper.

TORTA DI PEPE

Ingredients

grated cheese 50-80 g
fresh chard 1 bunch
olive oil 3-4 tbsp
ricotta 200 g
salt, pepper
milk 200 ml
flour 250 g
rice 200 g
nutmeg
eggs 2

Preparation

Mix the flour with a pinch of salt, olive oil and the water needed to obtain a soft and compact dough. Keep it in the refrigerator for 30 minutes.

Wash the chard, cut it into small pieces and boil it in water.

Also, in another pot, boil the rice in salted water prolonging the cooking for a few minutes beyond the usual cooking time (the rice must become very soft).

Heat the milk in a saucepan and add the ricotta, stirring to dissolve it.

Put the mixture of milk and ricotta in a bowl, add the drained rice and the finely chopped chard. Also add the grated cheese, grated nutmeg, salt and plenty of freshly ground black pepper.

Stir in the eggs, one at a time, mixing well to obtain a homogeneous filling to be used as a filling for the pepper cake.

Roll out the dough on a floured board and then place it in an oiled baking pan. Let the excess overflow out of the pan.

With a fork make a lot of tiny holes in the dough on the bottom of the baking pan. Then fill it in with the filling. Cover the filling with the dough surplass.

Sprinkle the surface with a little ground nutmeg, some more pepper and a drizzle of oil.

Bake at 200 ° C for about 30 minutes.

Take out the pepper cake and consume it cold or warm.

Notes: The pepper cake is the traditional savory pie of Camaiore, a town in the province of Lucca.

INSALATA DI CECI E TONNO

Ingredients

chickpeas 400-500 g
tuna (canned in oil) 2 cans
salad tomatoes 2-3
olive oil 4-5 tbsp
vinegar 1-3 tbsp
mustard 1-2 tsp
salt, pepper
onions 1-2
eggs 2

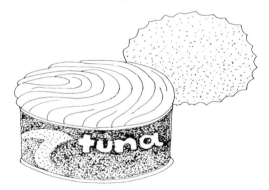

Preparation

Soak the chickpeas in water, overnight. Drain the chickpeas and boil them until they become really soft.

Boil the eggs and cut them into slices.

Peel and slice the tomatoes. Peel and then slice the onions.

In a bowl mix all the ingredients and then serve the salad.

GURGUGLIONE

Ingredients

red and yellow peppers 3-5
olive oil 4-5 tbsp
aubergines 1-2
tomatoes 3-6
potatoes 3-5
salt, pepper
zucchini 1-4
onions 1-3
basil

Preparation

Clean and then cut all the vegetables into fairly large pieces, about 3x3 cm in size.

In a suitable pot pour some olive oil. Add the onions first, and after a minute or two, also all the other vegetables, stir gently and cook over high heat. After a couple of minutes, lower the heat and continue cooking over moderate, later even low heat. Season with salt and pepper. When the dish is done, let it rest for 5-10 minutes before serving it.

Note: Gurguglione is a typical Elban dish, i.e. a dish belonging to the cuisine of the island of Elba, especially of the area of Rio Marina.

Numerous variants of the gurguglione exist, depending of the type of vegetables used.

CRESPELLE ALLA FIORENTINA

The batter of this type of crepes is the same as used for the sweet variant, but it is stuffed with ricotta and spinach. The filling may be a mixture of vegetables, but it may also be a meat filling. These crepes are generally garnished with a cream of béchamel or a tomato sauce.

FICATTOLA

The ficattola is a typical focaccia from the Tuscany region.

Although it can be sweet or savory, it is generally prepared as fried and salted bread dough, stuffed with salami (or ham) and cheese.

There is also the Prato and Mugello variant, with a slice of pancetta.

CECINA
(farinata di ceci)

Ingredients

chickpea flour 300 g
olive oil 6 tbsp
water 1.5 l
salt, pepper

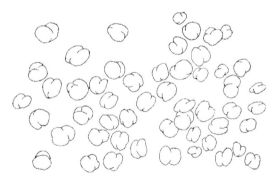

Preparation

Pour 1-1.2 liters of cold water into a bowl. With a whisk, gradually dissolve the chickpea flour in water, continuosly stirring.

Add the oil and some salt. Minced rosemary leaves, or thinly sliced and chopped onions, olives, dried tomatoes, pancetta or capers, can be added. Stir until the mixture is homogeneous, in fact still rather liquid, and then leave it to rest for 1-2 hours.

Grease a large baking pan with oil and pour in the cecina mixture. Cook the cecina in the oven at 200-230°C, for 15-25 minutes, until a light crust has been created on the surface.

Sprinkle the baked cecina with freshly ground pepper, maybe even some minced rosemary leaves.

Note: The cecina, or chickpea farinata, is a very low (about 0.5 cm) and round pie typical of Tuscany and Liguria, specially in the Pisa region.

La farifrittata is a frittata (fried mixture) prepared with the chickpea flour, with not so much water used as for a standard cecina.

Different name of the dish: torta (in the Livorno region).

Farinata gialla: In fact it is a polenta, prepared with corn flour, and cooked cannellini beans, or eggs.

CHAMPIGNON
ALLA
FIORENTINA

In a small saucepan, in some oil or butter, gently fry the chopped onion. Melt a knob of butter in a pan and add the boiled and squeezed spinach. In another pan, melt some butter, add the sliced champignons, salt them lightly and cook for 20 minutes. Grease a baking dish, spread the spinach on the bottom, spread over half of the onions, some grated cheese and a pinch of pepper. Then put the mushrooms, add the remaining onions, cheese and pepper. Bake in a hot oven at 180° for about 20 minutes.

CARNE

FINOCCHIONA "SBRICIOLONA"

Finocchiona is a typical Tuscan sausage made with minced pork, flavored with fennel seeds and dipped in red wine.

The "finocchiona" is produced in different parts of Tuscany and even in Lazio, but it is not the true and authentic "sbriciolona" that can be tasted only if you visit the Chianti area.

It is called sbriciolona because it crumbles easily while it is cut. It is very delicate on the palate, almost soft.

SOPRASSATA

The soprassata is a cured meat originating from Tuscany. It is produced of the head parts (tongue, cheek, cartilaginous parts) and the tail, all mixed with the rinds.

The soprassata is flavored with various spices, such as lemon or orange peel and parsley.

LARDO DI COLONNATA

The Lardo di Colonnata takes the name of the place located a few kilometers from Carrara.

It is produced with pork lard, rubbed with garlic, pepper, cinnamon, cloves, coriander, sage and rosemary.

PECORINO TOSCANO

Tuscan pecorino is a cheese made from sheep's milk. Depending on the area of production, the curing times change, the methods and with them the taste changes a lot.

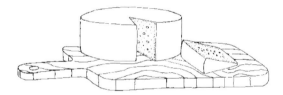

There are many variations of the standard Tuscan pecorino, all very tasty, such as: pecorino with chilli, pecorino with black pepper, pecorino matured in walnut leaves, etc.

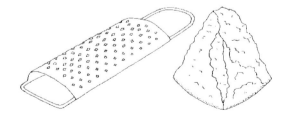

Among the Tuscan pecorino cheeses the most famous are those of Pienza and the Maremma.

POLLO ALLE ERBETTE

CHICKEN WITH HERBS

Ingredients

whole chicken 1 kg
dry white wine 100 tbsp
juniper berries
olive oil 4-5 t
salt, pepper
chili pepper
wild fennel
pennyroyal
rosemary
shallot
thyme
laurel
sage

Preparation

In a saucepan, gently fry in oil the chopped shallot. Add the crushed chili pepper and all the herbs, finely chopped. Cook for a few minutes, stirring frequently.

Then add the chicken (without the skin and cut into pieces). Season with salt and pepper. Pour the wine and continue cooking over medium heat for 30-40 minutes.

Optional additions: other types of meat - lamb, pork and veal, garlic, grated lemon peel, oregano, vegetable broth, stock cube, onion (instead of shallot), tomatoes.

Optional omissions: wild fennel, juniper berries, chilli, rosemary, pennyroyal, bay leaves, thyme or sage.

Optional procedure: Lightly flour the chicken pieces before frying them.

BISTECCA ALLA FIORENTINA

Ingredients

cut of the Chianina veal loin
1 - 1,8 kg
salt

Preparation

Put the meat on the grill, and roast it for app. 5 minutes (both sides). Salt the steak, and if you wish season it with pepper and olive oil, and serve it.

Suggestions: The steak should be mature, 15-21 days, maybe even longer.

Note: The Florentine steak is a cut of the calf's back, the calf being at least 24 months old, 3-4.5 cm high, of "Chianina" (or "maremmana") breed.

The shape of the steak should look like a heart, with the "T" shaped bone in the middle, with the meat fillets on both sides.

Warning: Remove the raw steak from

the refrigerator at least two hours before placing it on the embers.

ROSTICCIANA

Rosticciana (rostinciana) is a typical
Tuscan dish. It consists of pork chops
grilled on wood embers (or on a char-
coal fire).

Usually it is flavored only with pepper
and salt. But, it can also be seasoned
with different spices like rosemary.

ARISTA
ALLA
FIORENTINA

Ingredients

pork chine 1.5 kg
olive oil 5-6 tablespoons
garlic 1-3 cloves
salt and pepper
rosemary

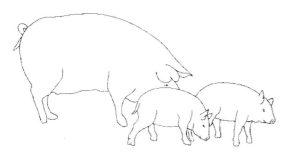

Preparation

With a small knife or a special tool
make the incisions in the meat. Season the pork loin with the mixture of
rosemary, fennel seeds, chopped
garlic, salt and pepper. Rub the surface of the meat with salt and ground
pepper. Sprinkle the meat with oil.

Cook the meat in the oven for 1.5-2.5
hours, at 130-180°C, turning it from
time to time and sprinkling it with the
cooking sauce.

Remove the roast and place it on a
cutting board. Let it rest for 15 minutes. Then remove the bone (optional),
cut the meat into slices and serve it
with the cooking sauce.

Optional ingredients: potatoes, added
about half an hour before the end of
cooking.

Spices and herbs: fennel seeds instead of rosemary, dry white wine, sage.

Optional proceeding: Brown the arista
in a saucepan in oil, before putting it
in a baking pan and in the oven.

Note: Today the arista is often prepared already boned, but it is advisable
to roast it with the bone. Detach the
meat partly from the bone, leaving it
attached only to a strip of meat. Season the bone with the mixture and
place the meat back on the bone.
Then bind the arista with the kitchen
string to keep it compact along the
cooking.

SCOTTIGLIA

Ingredients

mixed meat 1.5 kg
(veal, rabbit, pork, pigeon and
chicken, 300 g each)
ripe or peeled tomatoes 300-800 g
olive oil 4-5 tbsp
red wine 200 ml
garlic 1-2 cloves
salt, pepper
chili pepper
onions 2-3
parsley
basil

Preparation

Cut the meat into small pieces. Chop the peeled tomatoes. Finely chop the onion, garlic, parsley and basil.

Fry the onion and garlic in oil in a saucepan over low heat. When they start to brown, add the meat. Brown the meat over a high heat, turning it often. Pour a glass of red wine and let it evaporate over medium heat. Then add the tomatoes. Cover and continue cooking over low heat for 1-2 hours. Occasionally stir and add broth or water if the sauce gets too dry.

At the end of cooking, add the chili pepper and season with salt and pepper.

Optional ingredients: beef, feathered game, lamb, wild boar, duck, turkey, goose, ham, mortadella, salami, sausages, meat or bone broth, dry white wine instead of red wine, tomato passata in place of fresh or peeled tomatoes.

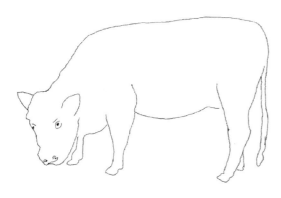

Spices and herbs: celery, carrot, lemon juice and peel, powdered vegetable broth, cinnamon, nutmeg, cloves, sage, bay leaf.

At the end you can prepare the scottiglia thick as the ragu or more soupy and serve it as a soup.

Note: This dish, typical of Tuscan cuisine, is also called "cacciucco di carne" or "cacciucco di terra", due to the many varieties of meat used together, just like the cacciucco di pesce.

STRACOTTO DI MANZO ALLA FIORENTINA
BEEF STEW, FLORENCE STYLE

Ingredients

beef 1.25 kg
pancetta (dried bacon) 60-80 g
ripe tomatoes 400-800 g
olive oil 4-5 tbsp
red wine 200 ml
garlic 1-2 cloves
salt, pepper
carrots 2-3
celery 1 rib
onions 1

Preparation

Cut one carrot into short sticks and the other into small cubes. Chop the onion, garlic and celery. Peel the tomatoes and cut them into pieces. Cut the pancetta (dried bacon) into short sticks.

Incise narrow holes in the meat and in some of them insert the carrot sticks and into others the pancetta sticks. Then tie up the meat with a kitchen string.

Warm up the oil. Fry the chopped onions, over low heat. Then add the celery, carrots and garlic. Stir a few times and lay down the meat. Raise the heat and brown the meat shortly all around. Then pour in the wine and let it almost evaporate. After that add the tomatoes, salt and pepper. Cook for 2-4 hours, over low heat.

Cut the meat into slices, not too thin. Season the meat slices with the meat sauce.

Optional herbs and spices: basil, garlic, nutmeg, cloves, tomato paste, vegetable bouillon powder.

PICCHIANTE

Ingredients

viel lungs ("picchiante") 500-700 g
dry white wine 70-150 ml
vegetable bouillon
powder or cube
olive oil 4-5 tbsp
garlic 1-3 cloves
tomatoes 1-4
potatoes 3-7
salt, pepper
onions 1-2
rosemary
carrot 1
sage

Preparation

In a pot, in some oil, gently fry the chopped onions. Later on, add the crushed garlic, grated carrot, chopped rosemary and sage leaves. Stir for a minute or two, over moderate heat.

After that, add the viel lungs, cut to pieces. Stir a couple or times and then pour in the wine. Cook until the wine is almost completely evaporated.

Then add the peeled and then chopped tomatoes, vegetable bouillon powder or cube. Season with salt and pepper. Soon, put in also the potatoes, cut to pieces. Continue cooking over medium heat, for 40-45 minutes.

Optional ingredients: viel heart, viel liver, viel meat, basil, bay leaves, vinegar, red wine, peperoncino.

IL PEPOSO

Ingredients

viel muscle meat 0.7-1 kg
red (Chianti) wine 0.5-1 l
(black) garlic 3-6 cloves
juniper berries 5-10
olive oil 4-5 tbsp
salt, pepper

Preparation

Put all the ingredients (meat cut in pieces, not too small, wine, berries, oil, garlic cloves, not peeled, salt, pepper in abundance) in an appropriate baking pan.

Put the pan in a preheated oven at 120°C, covering it with the lid.

Cook for 3-5 hours, checking from time to time that the meat does not dry too much during cooking. Only in this case add a little meat broth or water.

It is possible to replace the ground pepper with the pepper in grains, to get a more delicate dish but just as tasty.

Optional ingredients: tomatoes, onions, sage, rosemary, carrots, bay leaves, thyme, pepper in grains.

Optional: Before the further use, the meat may be marinated in the wine, seasoned with other ingredients, for 1-2 hours.

Note: The peposo is a typical Tuscan dish, originating from Impruneta. It is also called Peposo dell'Impruneta, Peposo all'imprunetina or Peposo dei fornacini dell'Impruneta, but also the Peposo alla fiorentina or Peposo dei fornaciai.

This ancient recipe was born around the year 1400 during the period in which the architect Filippo Brunelleschi was engaged in the construction of the dome of the Florence cathedral (Cattedrale di Santa Maria del Fiore or simply the Duomo). For the construction of the majestic dome an imposing production of terracotta was required which was produced in the Impruneta ovens.

Impruneta is a town in the Florentine hills, very famous for the "terra di Impruneta" (a clay containing sand, calcium carbonate and iron oxide, which gives the terracotta its characteristic reddish color), from which it is obtained terracotta, bricks and other terracotta materials (cotto d'Impruneta).

It was precisely the workers who cooked the bricks in the kilns (the Fornacini) who created this preparation. In a corner of the furnace, they started putting an earthenware pans with meat and all the other ingredients.

Statement: The Peposo dell'Impruneta is, without any doubt, considered to be the real essence of the Tuscan cuisine.

LAMPREDOTTO

Ingredients

lampredotto, already cleaned
600-700 g
8 slices of bread
or
4 large sandwiches cut in half
salt and pepper
chili pepper

and
for the broth:

tomatoes 3-4
onion 1 large
salt, pepper
carrots 2-4
parsley
celery

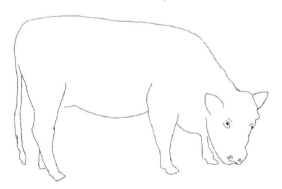

Preparation

Boil the lampredotto in plenty of salted water, with all the vegetables and aromatic herbs chosen for the broth, letting it to simmer slowly, for 1-2 hours.

eat and love Tuscany

Serve the lampredotto boiled, drained and cut into strips, accompanied with the so called "green sauce", or another type of sauce, the pickles or simply seasoned with salt and pepper.

Spices and herbs optional for the broth: garlic, basil, cloves.

Optional: Lampredotto can be served in sandwiches (panino al lampredotto). In fact the boiled lampredotto is also a street food. In Florence it is served by "lampredottai", or lampredotto sellers, called also the "trippai" in the sandwich bread (panino toscano) called "semelle", with the addition of the seasonings of choice (salt, pepper, green sauce (salsa di prezzemolo), spicy oil, etc.).

Note: Typical dish of the Florence cuisine.

The lampredotto is prepared boiling the "abomasum" of the veal.

Cattle have four stomachs. Three of these constitute the omasum, that part of the digestive system that breaks down the chemical plant bonds,

and the fourth, called abomasum, is in charge of the metabolization of food.

Unlike other Italian cities where the 4 stomachs of cattle are all called trippa, the tripe, in Florence, the 4 different names are kept and they are cooked in different ways, for each type of the tripe.

FEGATELLI

The fegatelli consist of pieces of pork liver wrapped in the pork net (omentum).

Cut the pork net into large square pieces and soak them in a bowl filled with warm water.

Divide the liver into 3 cm cubes.

In a bowl mix the breadcrumbs with a pinch of salt, a pinch of pepper, half a tablespoon of fennel seeds.

Roll the livers in the seasoning mix.

Wrap the livers each in a piece of the well-drained net. Fix the rolls with toothpicks, place them in an oiled baking pan and cook them quickly over medium heat. Or place the livers in skewers and cook them on the grill, brushing them with oil.

VITELLO TONNATO
VEAL
WITH TUNA FISH

Ingredients

veal 1 kg
canned tuna fish 150-250 g

desalted anchovy fillets 2-7
dry white wine 1-2 cups
olive oil 6-10 tbsp
garlic 1-2 cloves
capers 2-3 tbsp
bay leaves 1-5
cooked eggs 2
sale, pepe

Preparation

Cook the meat (uncut) in a pot, with the wine, oil, bay leaves, garlic, and salt and pepper, for 1-2 hours, over moderate heat. When and only if necessary, add some water.

Put the canned tuna fish meat into a bowl and add the chopped capers, anchovy fillets and cooked eggs, with some oil.

Slice the cooked meat and season them with the prepared tuna fish sauce.

Optional herbs and spices, while cooking the meat: onions, cloves, celery, vegetable bouillon powder, carrots, leeks, vinegar, rosemary.

Optional herbs and spices, while preparing the sauce: lemon zest and juice, egg yolks, mayonnaise (instead of cooked eggs).

Optional ingredients at the end: balsamic vinegar.

POLPETTE IN UMIDO
MEAT BALL STEW

Ingredients

ground pork 250 g
soft inside of a (thick) bread slice 1
tomato paste 1-3 tsp
(baby) beef 500 g
garlic 2-3 spicchi
olive oil 7-8 tbsp
bread crumbs
salt, pepper
cloves 2-5
onion 1-2
eggs 1-2
nutmeg
parsley

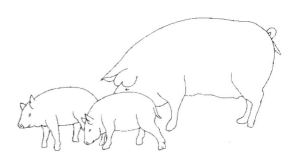

Preparation

In a bowl mix the ground meat, the eggs, the soft inside of a (thick) bread slice (already soaked in milk or water, and then squeezed out), the chopped garlic and parsley, the grated nutmeg, the salt and pepper, and the bread crumbs (adding it with caution).

Shape the meat balls and press them in the bread crumbs (or flour).

eat and love Tuscany

Then fry the meat balls in some oil, slightly and briefly, over medium heat.

In a pot warm up the oil and fry the chopped onions over low heat. Then add some bread crumbs, not much, and stir a few times, still over low heat. After that, stir in the tomato paste, the crushed cloves and a pinch of grated nutmeg. Lay down the meat balls in the pot (browned on the outside, but still raw inside). Pour in a cup of water, not covering the balls completely. Cook over moderate heat for 1-1.5 hours.

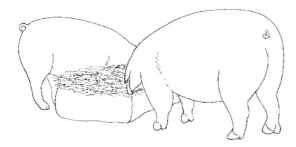

Optional ingredients of the meat ball mixture: grated cheese, fresh cheese, ricotta cheese, pancetta (dried bacon), mortadella, sausages, mushrooms, green olives, olives stuffed with red bell peppers or chili peppers, raisins soaked in water and squeezed out, pine nuts, grated carrots, vegetable bouillon powder, basil, paprika powder, chives, marjoram, sage, oregano, lemon or orange zest, capers, shallots, butter, wild fennel, flour, sugar, cinnamon, mustard, rice flakes, corn flour, milk, cream, grated cauliflower, ground almonds, mint, rosemary, cooked rice, fried onions, egg yolks instead of whole eggs, mozzarella o fior di latte cheese, ham, prosciutto ham, cooked potatoes.

Optional herbs and spices of the sauce: bread crumbs, pancetta (dried bacon), dry white wine, red wine, beer, dried mushrooms, grated carrots, garlic, basil, parsley, sweet wine, cream, mustard, vegetable bouillon powder, honey, cinnamon, rosemary, capers, mint, leeks, celery, bell peppers, potatoes, mushrooms, peas, lemon zest, sage.

POLPETTE ALLA LIVORNESE

MEAT BALLS, LIVORNO STYLE

Ingredients

ground veal meat 500-600 g
grated cheese 1-3 tbsp
garlic 1-2 cloves
breadcrumbs
potatoes 1-2
eggs 4-5
parsley

Preparation

Boil the potato and then peel it and crush it.

In a bowl mix the ground meat, the crushed potatoes, grated cheese and the minced parsley and garlic. Shape the meat balls and pass them in the breadcrumbs.

Once this is done, fry the meat balls in a pan with a little oil.

Optional ingredients: thyme, onions.

INVOLTINI DI CARNE

MEAT ROLLS

Ingredients

pork or veal slices 1 kg
pancetta (dried bacon) or prosciutto
ham 150-200 g
soft inside of a bread slice 1
butter or olive oil 4-5 tbsp
grated cheese 100-150 g
dry white wine 100 ml
egg 1 or egg yolks 1-2
ground meat 100 g
garlic 1-3 cloves
salt, pepper
nutmeg
parsley
flour

Preparation

In a bowl mix the soft inside of a bread slice (previously soaked in water or milk and then squeezed out), chopped prosciutto ham, garlic and parsley, egg (or yolks), ground meat, grated cheese, grated nutmeg, salt and pepper.

Spread a thin layer of the prepared mixture over each meat slice (previously pounded if necessary). Roll tightly the meat slices and fasten them with toothpicks.

Press the meat rolls in flour and then

fry them for a couple of minutes. After that pour in the wine and let it almost evaporate, still over medium heat. Then pour in some water and continue cooking for 30-45 minutes.

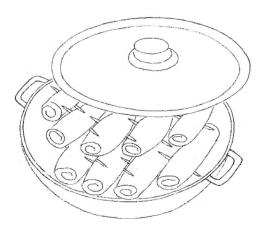

Optional ingredients of the filling: chicken livers, sausage, mortadella, bread crumbs instead of bread.

Optional herbs and spices of the sauce: rosemary, vegetable bouillon powder.

Possible omissions: ground meat.

COSTOLETTE AL ROSMARINO

CUTLETS WITH ROSEMARY

Ingredients

veal, pork or lamb cutlets 1 kg
dry white wine 200-300 ml
olive oil or butter 4-5 tbsp
(fresh) rosemary
salt

Preparation

Warm up the oil in a pan. Brown brie-

eat and love Tuscany

fly the cutlets and then season with chopped rosemary and salt. Pour in the wine and continue cooking for 5-6 minutes.

Optional ingredients: peas or potatoes, cooked but not thoroughly, butter.

Optional ingredients: garlic, carrots, celery, parsley, dry white or red wine, rosemary, pancetta (dry bacon), breadcrumbs, concentrated tomato paste, basil, vinegar, sage, lemon juice and/or peel, bey leaves.

Note: At the end, the dish may be prepared containing more or less liquid (trippa in umido or trippa al sugo), salsiccia.

TRIPPA
ALLA
FIORENTINA

Ingredients

tripe 1 kg
fresh mature tomatoes,
peeled tomatoes or passata
200-500 g
olive oil 4-5 tbsp
salt, pepper
onions 1-2

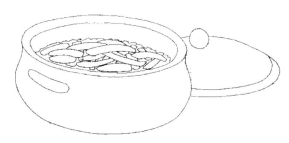

Preparation

Cut the already cooked tripe in strips.

In a pot, in olive oil, gently fry the chopped onions. Then add the peeled and minced tomatoes. Cook over moderate heat. Season with salt and pepper.

Serve sprinkled with grated Parmesan and a drizzle of olive oil.

FRITTATA
CON GLI ZOCCOLI

The frittata with zoccoli is an omelette enriched with bacon cubes, or fresh meat or cured meat, cut to pieces. Bread cubes, thinly cut potatoes or onions may be added, too.

CINGHIALE
IN DOLCEFORTE
WILD BOAR, SWEET AND STRONG

Ingredients

wild boar meat in pieces 1-1,25 kg
dark chocolate 25-30 g
red wine 200-500 ml
olive oil 4-5 tbsp
garlic 2-3 cloves
vinegar 1 tbsp
salt, pepper
carrots 1-2
onions 1-2
cloves 3-4
rosemary
thyme
celery
laurel

Preparation

Put the wild boar in a bowl with the

wine, vinegar, aromatic herbs, carrot, onion and celery cut into small pieces and the crushed cloves. Marinate for 12 hours.

After this time, pour some olive oil into a pan, add the crushed garlic and brown the well drained pieces of marinated meat, adding new herbs to the pan.

Stir well, add salt and pepper and the remaining seasonings. Pour in the wine from the marinade.

Cook for about 1,5 hours, covered with the lid. Add some water if and when it is necessary. A couple of minutes before the end of cooking, stir in the grated chocolate.

Optional ingredients: cinnamon, bay leaves, pine nuts, raisins.

CINGHIALE IN SALMÌ

WILD BOAR IN BRINE

Ingredients

wild boar meat in pieces 1-1,25 kg
red wine 400-500 ml
olive oil 4-5 tbsp
garlic 1-3 cloves
juniper berries
carrots 1-2
onions 1-2
bay leaves
cloves 3-5
rosemary
celery
sage
salt

Preparation

Rinse the wild boar meat and put it in a bowl full of salted water. Change the salted water a few times during the day, app. every three hours.

In the evening drain the meat and put it into another bowl. Season it with grated carrots, chopped celery and onions, juniper berries, cloves, cinnamon, chrushed garlic, sage, bay leaves and rosemary. Then cover the meat with wine. Let the meat soak in the marinade, in the refrigerator, until tomorrow.

Drain the meat from the marinade and dab it well with a sheet of kitchen paper. Cut into 3 cm cubes.

In a pot in some oil gently fry the chopped, crushed and minced herbs, new ones, not the filtered ones from the marinade.

Add the wild boar and brown it well. Continue cooking for 15-20 minutes. Add two bay leaves and some rosemary. Pour in the remaining wine, not used in the marinade, and continue cooking over low heat for 2-3 hours, until the meat is tender.

If the cooking liquid should dry up, pour in some broth or water. Season with salt and pepper, and with olive oil. Serve the meat with its sauce, accompanied by mashed potatoes, polenta or pasta.

eat and love Tuscany

IL CIBREO

Ingredients

chicken livers 500 g
olive oil 2-3 tbsp
butter 2-3 tbsp
half a lemon
salt, pepper
egg yolks 2
onion 1
flour
sage

Preparation

In a pan, in olive oil, gently fry the chopped onions. Add the floured livers, cut in pieces, sage, salt and pepper.

Cook over medium heat for 10-15 minutes, adding some water or chicken broth, when needed.

After that, remove the pan from the heat, adding the egg yolks (previously beaten) and the lemon juice.

After letting the sauce rest for a few minutes, it can be served on slices of Tuscan bread, better if toasted.

Note: Cibreo is a typical dish of the Florentine tradition.

CONIGLIO IN PORCHETTA

Ingredients

rabbit 1
dry white wine 100-150 ml
sliced ham 150-200 g
vinegar 200-250 ml
olive oil 4-5 tbsp
garlic 1-2 cloves
butter 1-2 tbsp
bay leaves 1-3
salt, pepper
wild fennel
rosemary
sage

Preparation

Bone the rabbit and let it marinate for at least an hour in cold water and vinegar. Then drain the rabbit, pass it under running water and then dry it.

Chop the sage, rosemary, fennel and garlic, put half of it on the open boned rabbit and sprinkle with pepper. Place the ham slices on top and spread the rest of the chopped herbs.

Roll the rabbit as tightly as possible, and tie the roll with the kitchen string.

In an pot, warm up some olive oil with a knob of butter, brown the rabbit, turning it several times. Then pour in the wine, let it almost evaporate, add the bay leaves, an cover the pot. Cook for at least 90 minutes, adding some water if necessary. Remove it, let it cool for a while, remove the string and cut the roll into slices.

BUGLIONE

Ingredients

lamb, hare, chicken or wild boar meat
1-1,5 kg

tomatoes, fresh, peeled or passata
200-300 g
peperoncino (chili pepper)
dry white wine 50-80 ml
red wine 400-500 ml
olive oil 4-5 tbsp
vinegar 1 tbsp
bay leaves 1-3
garlic 2 cloves
salt, pepper
cloves 2-3
rosemary
carrot 1
onion 1
celery
sage

Preparation

Put the meat in a bowl with the wine red wine, vinegar, aromatic herbs, carrot, onion and celery cut into small pieces and the crushed cloves. Marinate for 12 hours.

In a pot, in olive oil, gently fry the chopped onions. Add the crushed garlic and chopped rosemary and sage leaves. Then add the drained meat.

After a couple of minutes of frying the meat, pour in the white wine. Cook over medium heat until the wine almost evaporates.

Then add the tomatoes. Continue cooking over moderate heat, for quite a few hours, until the meat is tender.

Serve the buglione with toasted Tuscan bread.

Optional ingredients: diced pancetta.

Notes: The buglione is a typical dish of the Tuscan gastronomic tradition and in particular of the area of Capalbio and surroundings.

FRITTATINE IN TRIPPA

Ingredients

fresh eggs 6
grated cheese 50-60 g
tomato passata 100-200 g
toasted bread slices 6
olive oil 3-4 tbsp
aglio 1 clove
salt

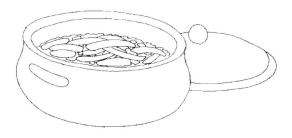

Preparation

In a bowl, beat the eggs with a pinch of salt.

In a pan warm up some olive oil, pour the beaten eggs and fry an omelette. Then remove the omelette from the stove and cut it into strips, like those of tripe.

Warm up the oil in a pan, add the garlic and then the tomato sauce, After 10 minutes, add the strips of omelette, stirring gently, letting them to absorb the sauce. Sprinkle with grated cheese, cover and cook for another 2-3 minutes.

Transfer everything to the serving dish, with the slices of toasted bread.

LA TEGAMATA DI PITIGLIANO

Ingredients

viel meat 0,8-1 kg
fresh or peeled tomatoes
400-500 g
red wine 100-120 ml
potatoes 500-700 g
olive oil 4-5 tbsp
salt, pepper
rosemary
carrot 1
onion 1
cloves

Preparation

Cut the meat into cubes and put it in a marinade with red wine, carrot, chopped onion, rosemary and cloves.

Tomorrow morning, drain the pieces meat and keep the marinade liquid aside.

In a pot warm up some olive oil and put in the drained meat. Fry it, stirring from time to time. Soon start adding a spoonful or two of the saved marinade. After 5-10 minutes of cooking over medium heat, put in the tomatoes, and, 5-10 minutes later, also the potatoes.

Continue cooking over moderate heat until the meat is tender, as well as the potatoes.

Note: This dish is typical in the region of Pitigliano, a town in the province of Grosseto.

BRASATO AL BRUNELLO DI MONTALCINO

Ingredients

beef or viel meat 2 kg
olive oil 4-5 tbsp
pepper in grains
parsley
salt

for the marinade

Brunello di Montalciano wine 1 l
carrots 2-3
bay leaves
onions 2
pepper
celery

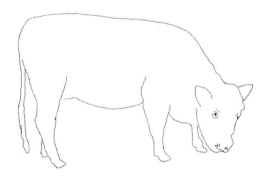

Preparation

Chop the onions and carrots and dice the celery. Put the meat in a bowl and cover it with the marinade prepared with wine, vegetables, bay leaves, pepper grains and garlic. Let it soak for 24 hours. Then drain the meat.

Brown the meat in a casserole in the olive oil. Add the marinade liquid with the drained vegetables, and season with salt and pepper.

Cook all together for a few minutes over a high heat.

Cover the casserole and place it, with the braised meat in the preheated oven. Cook the meat for about two and a half hours, maybe longer.

When the meat is cooked, cut it into slices, sprinkle with the prepared sauce and the chopped parsley.

ROVELLINA ALLA LUCCHESE

Slices of beef, breaded (with flour, eggs and breadcrumbs) and fried, and after that seasoned with tomato sauce, prepared with onions, garlic, parsley, oregano and capers, by shortly cooking the fried meat slices in the tomato sauce, over low heat.

POLLO ALLA DIAVOLA

Ingredients

chicken meat 1 kg
peperoncino (chili pepper)
olive oil 4-5 tbsp
garlic 1-2 cloves
vinegar 1 tbsp
salt, pepper
rosemary
lemon 1

Preparation

Prepare a sauce with olive oil, rosemary, garlic, lemon peel, salt, pepper, chili pepper and vinegar.

Add the chicken meat in and let it cook, over moderate heat, until the meat is tender.

If and when it is necessary, pour in some dry white wine, vegetable soup or water.

GRIFI

The grifi are the parts of the chianina calf snout, cooked with onions, concentrated tomato paste, red wine, thyme and cloves.

There is also a street food version: the pan co'grifi (a sandwich stuffed with the grifi and their sauce).

Note: Among the typical dishes of Arezzo, the famous "grifi all'aretina" deserve a special mention.

MATUFFI

The matuffi are a rustic preparation of Lucca origin.

This is a dish composed of layers of creamy (not firm) polenta alternating with layers of a meat sauce.

Tasty variations are the matuffi with porcini mushrooms or with wild boar sauce.

COOKING
TIPS

The first and the utmost important step, even before the beginning of the cooking process, is to purchase only the first quality ingredients, as fresh as possible.

The secret why some dishes taste better than others lies not only in the balance of the components used, but also in the sequence and the timing when they are to be added during the process of cooking a dish.

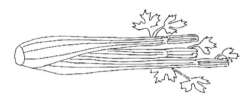

Do not put too many different herbs and spices into the food you are preparing.

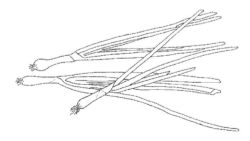

Add the seasonings gradually, tasting the food more than once in order to balance the flavours.

Do not rush and do not overheat in order to speed up the cooking process. The slow cooking of food deeply enhances its flavour.

Your creativity in the process of preparing food is always welcome. But, at the same time, do not forget to honor the fact that the basic recipe usually reflects the centuries lasting effort of our predecessors to find the perfect taste of the dish.

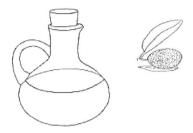

A chosen sauce for pasta or rice sometimes may be prepared not only by warming up the ingredients during the process but also by mixing and blending without heating.

Never cover the pan in which you cook a sauce.

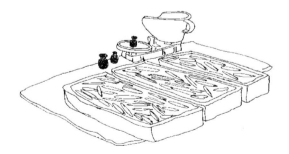

The preparation of a meal does not start on the stove, but with the selection of fresh and appropriate food.

CUCINA TOSCANA

Dalle colline   From the hills,
coperte d'ulivi   covered with olive trees,
e da montagne   and from the mountains,
muschiose, solitarie mossy, solitary and still silent,
e ancora silenziose, like those of Tuscany,
come quelle della Toscana, which kitchen
quale cucina   do you like to come out?
volete che esca?   From here
Di qui non può che uscire no other than
una tavola rustica   a rustic and yet refined cuisine
e però raffinata.   can appear.

Anna Gosetti della Salda

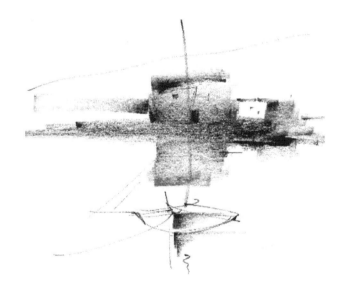

ITALIAN
FOOD

Italian food is seasonal.
It is simple.
It is nutritionally sound.
It is flavorful.
It is colorful.
It's all the things
that make for a good eating experience,
and
it's good for you.

Lidia Bastianich

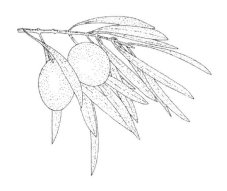

Quotes and aphorisms

''Some people ask the secret of our long marriage. We take time to go to a restaurant two times a week. A little candlelight, dinner, soft music and dancing. She goes Tuesdays, I go Fridays.'' Henny Youngman

"Forgive me, love! No! No! It is not true that you are not a good cook. Lately the cold buttered spaghetti were always cold to the right point! "
Rocco Barbaro

''When the waitress asked if I wanted my pizza cut into four or eight slices, I said ''Four. I don't think I can eat eight.'' Yogi Berra

I said "Where do you want to go for your anniversary?" She said: "I want to go somewhere I've never been before." I said "Try the kitchen."
Henny Youngman

'' The cake must always be remarkable because it comes
after you're no longer hungry. ''Alexandre Grimod

''The man also eats with his eyes, especially if the waitress is pretty.''
Ugo Tognazzi

"A recipe is a story that always ends with a good meal.
But when I cook, the end becomes uncertain.'' Pat Conroy

"I always cook with wine, sometimes I even add it to the food." W.C. Fields

"Italians have only two things on their mind. The other one is spaghetti."
Catherine Deneuve

''The trouble with eating Italian food is that three or four days later you're hungry again.'' George Miller

''I have removed all the bad food from the house. It was delicious.''

INDEX

Printed in Great Britain
by Amazon